Arcadia
Story From Another Time

by Ben Dale

To my wife, Michelle, who can now have in written form all the stories from my Mission that she has heard again, and again, and again, and…you get the idea.

And to my kids Bronwyn, CJ, Katie, Jake, Joe, and Christina; so that my grandkids, and my great grandkids, and my great-great…you get the idea…

…so they know what I went through.

Story Guide

A Light and a Voice	1
Not Quite Converted	6
A Testimony Is Born	12
Goooooooooool!	23
First Miracle	26
Feels Like The First Time	31
Into The Fire	36
The Hooker	41
The Ranger	47
The Pastor	52
The Wolves	55
The Girl	59
Bullet	63
Gordon Jump, Cow-Eye Soup…	65
DeFiguerido	69
The Ride	73
The Jerk	76
November '86	80
Thanksgiving	84
Frequent Stops	87
Confessions Of A District Leader	90
A Vision	94
Holidays	97
Zone 7	102
Del Rio	104
Tamales	107
Mission Barber	108
Final Four	113
Hard-Headed	115
Super Missionaries	118
The Ugliness	119
Different Guy	123
A Sign	127
Attwooll	129

Story Guide

Close Call	133
Planting Seeds	140
Never Get Out of the Boat	144
Same Old Song And Dance	150
President Coleman	153
Buchanan	156
The Right Stuff	158
Mortensen	161
Dime-Shaped Object	165
Best Decision Ever	167
Curses Removed	173
Dogs Dogs Dogs	181
The Hard Times	187
J-Dubs	191
The Car	195
Bad News	198
Butterfly Knife	201
Dummy	204
Great And Spacious Building	207
Sister Tucker, González, Badál, Calderón, and Hinojosa	211
Ramiro	215
Near Beer	218
Golden Gloves	219
Super Bowl	222
Music	224
Trunky	226
Going Home	232
Story For Another Time	233
Perceptions	234
Epilogue by Elder Jim Ashworth	236
On *becoming*	238
On the Term *Mormon*	240

The ability to **become** is what separates us from the other animals

Nicholas Edward Dale, and his wife Sarah Ann Keye arrived on the ship *Horizon* in Jamestown in 1624. They left Yorkshire where Nicholas' parents George and Sarah, his grandparents Jefferye and Jane, and his great grandparents Nicholas and Anne had lived since 1510. Nicholas was 23, and Sarah was 19, and pregnant with their first son Thomas, who would be the first Dale born in the Colonies.

There are indications the baby Thomas was named after Nicholas' uncle, the famous Sir Thomas Dale. Nicholas and Sarah bought, or acquired, 75 acres along the Charles River in the area now called Richmond, Virginia.

They grew tobacco.

A Light and a Voice

"We're Mormons, it's what we do." - Gram.

I cannot remember a time in my life when this wasn't the refrain. Growing up Mormon, there was never a time when I was given a choice as to what to do with my religion. On Sundays, we went to church. On Wednesdays, we went to Boy Scouts. On Saturdays, we went camping as scouts during the day, then to church dances at night. I did all of the ordinance-advancements (baptism, priesthood, church callings - jobs) without question…and all this was okay. It was simply what we did. I even graduated from Seminary…a sort of Bible school, though I did not learn much. My teacher, Sister

May was amazing, but I was lazy, and not that into it. Coming from "pioneer stock," there was always the scepter of a century-long tradition hanging over every choice and decision. All that was okay, too.

It's just what we did.

When I turned 19, it came time to go to the Temple and go on a Mission. I did all this without question also. The Temple can be pretty intense, especially if your knowledge of the Church is limited. The experience was startling for me, but I bore it all quietly. It's just what we did. There's nothing wrong with the Temple ceremonies…in fact I find them to be uplifting and peaceful, but it is a very different experience than what a congregate gets on Sunday in a chapel service.

I put in my mission papers soon thereafter and awaited my assignment from Salt Lake. I told people that "the Spirit" told me I was going to Austria; so, when the Call came to Arcadia, I claimed to have misheard what I was told. The two words seemed close enough to claim a simple misunderstanding.

I actually met President Benson, the Prophet of the Church at the time, just before receiving my mission assignment or "Call". He visited his "home Ward" in Bethesda, Maryland while I was working as a congressional intern. I shook his hand and greeted him, awestruck. He met my warmth, and when I told him my papers were in, he looked me up and down and said, "Well, you're a Call and a haircut away."

I went to the barber that week.

After receiving my mission call, I had to wait about four months before departing for the California Arcadia Mission (Spanish-speaking). I spent that time working to make as much money as I could. Mormon Missionaries do not receive money for serving. Astonishingly to many, missionaries pay to be out there serving…pretty remarkable.

The Lord also had a plan to get me ready.

One night, while lying in bed, I was half-asleep when suddenly I was wide-awake, but unable to move. I was completely paralyzed, but absolutely lucid and aware. My eyes were open, but I had the sensation of being inside my skull, looking out through my eye sockets, as though I was in a room looking out through windows.

I was in this state for a period of time, not hours, but long enough to wonder what in the actual heck was going on. Eventually, my point of view returned to my eyes like normal, but I still couldn't move. At the same time that my sight normalized, I became aware that my room was completely black…not a darkness, but a blackness as though everything in the room had been painted over. My eyes were open, and I could "see," but there was nothing to see.
Nothing.

At the moment I processed all this, I became aware of a point of light, directly above my head. I had to arch my neck back to be able to look up enough to see it. The light was a diamond-shaped hole coming through the black background. It was very fine…the word I would most use to describe the light, whenever reflecting on this, is "precise." The light coming through was small, but very precise.

As soon as I was able to process what was happening, I heard a voice, that seemed to come from the same precise hole as the light. "Do you feel that?," it said. I figured the question referred to my inability to move, so I concentrated hard in order to think the word, "yes." It took some effort to concentrate on the response, while quieting down my brain trying to process everything that was happening.

Again, the question:
"Do you feel that?"
"Yes"
"That's the power of the Adversary…" The *Adversary* is another

name for Satan.

The voice continued, "when this happens, here is what you do: raise your right arm to the square." This took some effort, because I couldn't move. I'm not sure if I was actually doing it, but in my mind, my right arm was raised, making a square…kind of like making a right-hand turn signal from a car window, but with your right arm.

After I was convinced this was done, the voice said, now repeat after me: "By the power of the Holy Melchizedek Priesthood, and in the name of Jesus Christ, get thee hence." When I had repeated the phrase, I immediately regained control of my body.

I stayed lying on my bed, face up, but brought my right arm down to my side. The light was still there, and as soon as I looked at it, I again lost the ability to move physically.
The voice again said:
"Do you feel that?"
"Yes."
"That's the power of the Adversary. When this happens, raise your arm to the square, and say: By the power of the Holy Melchizedek Priesthood, and in the name of Jesus Christ, get thee hence. Do it now."

When I did as instructed, the ability to move returned. I was relieved and scared in equal measure. As soon as I had these thoughts, it happened again.
"Do you feel that?"
"Yes.
"That's the power of the Adversary. From now on, and throughout your life, you will need to know what to do when this

 For more on Mormon Pioneers

happens to you, or when you see it happen to others. Do you know what to do?"

"Yes."

"Do it now."

I raised my arm to the square and said, "By the power of the Holy Melchizedek Priesthood, and in the name of Jesus Christ, get thee hence." I immediately regained control of my body. When I looked up, the light was gone, and looking around, though dark, I could see normally in the room again.

I don't have any explanation for what happened that night other than retelling the story here, but what I can tell you is: I would need to use what I was taught in that lesson many many times.

A few weeks later, I got on a plane bound for Provo, Utah, and the MTC.

For more on Melchizedek Priesthood

Dales were all farmers.

Thomas Dale, along with his wife, Judith Van Renesse, continued the tradition of growing tobacco in Virginia for generations…through Reuben Thomas Dale and Rebecca Elizabeth Simmons, to their son Abraham Delaware Dale and Winifred Southern, to their son William Dale and Frances Phillips, to their son William Dale and Margaret E. Mabe, for a total of six generations.

By the early 1780s, William and Margaret moved to land in Tennessee that had been granted the family for William's service in George Washington's Continental Army.

William owned wagons, and survived Valley Forge.

Not Quite Converted

Pulling up to the Missionary Training Center or MTC, I had no idea what to expect. The only thing I can remember is how I felt. There is no feeling like being a new missionary. There is a mixture of wonder, fear, accomplishment, excitement, and an overwhelming foreboding. My pals from Alpine, Utah, Cliff Nielsen and the Hickenlooper brothers (Brett and Bart) were there. That was good and bad. Good, in the sense that I didn't feel so alone. Bad, in the sense that they were my pals from the outside, and I needed to focus on being a missionary on the inside. Being around my pals just made me want to goof off and party. We were all going to different places around the world, so in the end we didn't see each other that much.

Brett   Cliff   Me   Bart

When you get to the MTC, they divide you up into groups of 8-12 missionaries called Districts. I was put into the Montebello District, and assigned Elder Joyce as my companion. He was a nice enough guy, a little quirky, and not my type of dude. He didn't know anything about sports. What made it livable was Elder Joyce was the only guy in our District not going to Arcadia. I can't remember where he was going, but I want to say somewhere in South America. We were put into a room with two bunk beds along with Elders Buchanan and Gardner. Elder Martin was also with our group and we were all going to Arcadia, along with two sisters, Downs and Pearce.

Left to Right:
Buchanan, Gardner, Me, Joyce, Martin

For those of you new to the game, "Elder" is both a title and an office. In the case of missionaries, it's both. Missionaries hold the advanced, or Melchizedek Priesthood, and hold the office of an Elder. But saying Elder so-and-so is how male missionaries are addressed. We would constantly be asked our first names; always responding, "uh…Elder." I never knew a companion's first name until they were long gone. Missionary "companions" are simply two missionaries assigned to each other. You will never…ever…see a missionary alone. It is forbidden.

Sister missionaries do not hold a priesthood office, and are referred to as "Sister so-and-so." They also serve in pairs, called companionships.

As for my MTC companions, Elder Buchanan was fun-loving, jovial, and jolly. We shared a similar sense of humor and gravitated toward each other. Gardner had an air of General Authority (world leader) about him. He was a great guy, really nice, but very serious and wanted to be the absolute best missionary and Mormon. I always liked him, but I always felt like I didn't measure up when I was around him. Martin was quiet, and had left a serious girlfriend back home.

Only a few months after arriving in Arcadia, I heard that Elder Martin went home. A missionary going home "early" is a stressful event for the missionary's family, as well as for the missionary's Ward. In those days, you did not just go home. It happened, but it was very rare. There was, and still is to a much lesser degree, an amount of shame in returning home early. A Mission is two years, and the expectation is that you serve the entire time. The shame was not only on the missionary, but on the entire family as well. Parents took it as failure on their part. Trust me, members of the Church reading this are uncomfortable right now. That's ok…we should talk about it openly. It is a cultural problem with the <u>people</u> in the Church. If this was the era of the Apostle Paul, he would surely write an epistle admonishing us all about this stupid part of our culture.

The good news is: there is much more…MUCH more understanding and empathy for families and missionaries who do not complete their time. It's one of the great things about us as a people. We do show an ability to evolve.

When I heard about Martin going home to marry that girl, my thought (though unexpressed to anyone else) was, "good for him." I was happy for him. He realized the Mission wasn't for him. He loved that girl, and he went home to marry her. What's so wrong with that? Nothing, in my view.

At the MTC, we worshipped (admired deeply) our instructors, Elders Romney and Jackson. They seemed so old and mature, but in reality, they were probably in their early to mid-20s. They had three roles: teach us Spanish, teach us how to teach, and help us gain even stronger testimonies of the Gospel of Jesus Christ. I can remember wanting to be like them so badly, and wanting them to be proud of me.

We spent our days in class. Eight hours or more learning Spanish, and learning how to teach. We had intermittent breaks during the day: once to go to the gym, where I learned Mormon guys can ball; three times to eat meals that were all protein and carbs; and once in the evening for devotionals. General Authorities would come down daily from Salt Lake to talk to us. My most memorable were Elders Marvin J. Ashton, Dallin H. Oaks, and Thomas S. Monson. The talk given by Elder Ashton made me want to run though a brick wall for the Lord. Elder Monson, who would later become Prophet/President, made me feel an immense pride to serve. I was also a missionary leader by the time of Elder Monson's visit, so I got to have lunch with him. We asked him a ton of questions. Mine was, "What's the most important tool for a missionary?" His response, "A strong testimony of the divinity of Jesus Christ and His Restored Church." That answer would haunt me mentally for the next few months.

All in all, the MTC was a wonderful experience, but I was still living with one foot in the world. To me, the missionary dorms were one big frat house, and I played the role of John "Bluto" Blutarsky. It was one big party to me. I was living my best life.

Since that time, and many others like them, I have reflected on why I have to be the center of attention. The quick answer is a narcissistic need to be in the center. But I don't think that's it. The reality is, and bear with me, that it's all a reaction to being an introvert. NOW, anyone who knows me cannot believe I just tried to claim that I'm an introvert, but I am. If there is time in my schedule, I prefer to be alone. Write music, watch a show, exercise, do other projects around the house. I'm fine by myself. A loner.

If my wife announces, and she frequently does, that we are going to some party somewhere with people I don't know, I'd rather be hit in the head with a ball peen hammer. I try to hide my unwillingness to go, but I'm sure Michelle knows, though she's nice enough not to scold me about it.

So we go to the party, and what do I do? Instead of

What is a General Authority?

hiding in the corner, which I know is not an option, I go the other direction. Having been raised among first ballot Hall of Fame story tellers on both sides of the family, I go into a "holding court," center of attention-mode. If I can get everyone cracking up and listening to all the crazy stories I have in a mental file, then I don't have to deal with the horror and awkwardness of having to be there. It's like people who face their fears by dedicating their lives to running straight at the thing. We find out in *The West Wing* that the reason Admiral Percy Fitzwallace joined the Navy, eventually becoming Chair of the Joint Chiefs, is because of the paralyzing fear he felt when his father took him sailing as a child.

That's me. I end up dominating a room socially, because I'm dreading and terrified to be there. Analyze THAT!

Nevertheless, at the MTC, the only time I felt lonely was one day in the gym. We were all on the floor stretching before a brutal full court session, when one of the missionary trainers gave us an update on March Madness 1986…I was missing out. I still had one foot in the world.

After eight weeks of intense language and Gospel training, we were ready to be turned loose on the good people of Southern California. I left with a sense of preparedness… in the MTC, I read the Book of Mormon from cover to cover for the first time, not an approach I'd recommend to prospective missionaries, and certainly nothing to brag about. At the time, I was very proud of the accomplishment, but time, experience, and maturity have educated me on the ludicrous idea of going to preach about a book I had never read.

The MTC President gave me a priesthood blessing right before we left for California. Any priesthood blessing, whether it be for healing, counsel, or comfort involves someone with the Melchizedek Priesthood placing their hands on your head and saying only what God inspires to be said. In this blessing, the MTC President said, "if you will dedicate yourself to reading the

Book of Mormon, the Spanish language will come easy to you for the rest of your life. You will master it without ever opening a grammar text." That came true.

Later in life I would MAX (perfect score) the Defense Language Exam in Spanish without ever having opened a grammar or language textbook.

Dales were always looking West.

After generations in Virginia, the Dales would keep moving. William and Margaret settled near Overton, Tennessee and began farming. They had numerous children; one of whom, Alexander, would marry Leah Horner. Their son, Joshua Dale, married Rachael Shipley, and moved to a farm near Harrison, Missouri. Their son, Benjamin, married Mary Louisa Lindsey, and they moved to Great Bend, Kansas, where my great grandfather, Elmer Lewis Dale, was born in 1875.

In a civil dispute over dairy products, Benjamin would be described as "lazy and shiftless," and that his horses and cattle were wasted on such a bum.

In spite of the public evisceration, he loved Mary; he died, only hours after she did, from a broken heart. The local paper described them both as "religiously devout until the end."

A Testimony Is Born

Arriving in California felt like a dream. I was now out in public wearing THE uniform…dark suit, white shirt, dark shoes, and plain tie. The missionary badge or placard seemed to pulsate, hanging over my left breast suit pocket. People stared as we walked, and I didn't know what to do. Do I stop and talk to everyone? Do I walk quickly and hope no one talks to me? We got our bags, and were met at the curb by two missionaries who looked disheveled. They were the A.P.s, or Assistants to the President, and their look came from hard work and washing their own clothes for two years. I remember noticing their shoes were trashed. Yet, they had a maturity and wisdom about them in the form of an aura that made you feel safe. I instantly wanted to be like them. We piled into the van and headed to the Mission President's house in Arcadia. Exiting the airport, I saw my first strip club. The famous Nudes, Nudes, Nudes sign just outside of LAX. I didn't know I was "country," but yes, I was country. We all pretended to not look at the sign.

When we arrived at President Meier's house, he and his wife were standing out in the yard to greet us; which in retrospect, is strange in the pre-cell phone era. I loved them both immediately. If you want to imagine what they looked like, imagine an off-season Mr. and Mrs. Santa Claus.

They had a warmth to them that only comes from tending to the needs of young LDS missionaries. They beckoned us inside.

By comparison, our incoming group of missionaries was small. There were only six of us. Over my years in the Mission, I'd see new groups of well over 20 come in at one time. We immediately had dinner…supper really…as it was early. We had time to take a nap and then walk the neighborhood, which was fun; Arcadia neighborhoods are a refuge to peacocks that just roam around the yards, sidewalks and streets. Later that afternoon, the trainers showed up.

My missionary trainer was Elder William Widdup. Trainers are trusted missionary veterans who introduce new missionaries or "greenies" to missionary work. Mine had a hairline that made him look older than he was, and he greeted me like he planned to train me hard. Good news was: he was a District Leader (first-level leader over 4-5 pairs of missionaries) in Zone 7, serving in Burbank, so he had a car. District Leaders all have cars, because they have to travel to other areas to serve and support other missionaries assigned to their District. So…I didn't have to buy a bike, or so I thought.

My first pad in Burbank. My room was the behind the lower left window.

Elder Widdup said that I'd needed a bike to go on "splits." Once assigned to another missionary, the pair or companionship stay together 24 hours a day until one or both receive a transfer to another companionship or area. Yet, from time to time the companionship will split for a day to go with another missionary. So, I needed a bike. Being boojie from birth, I bought a Bianchi road racer that would pretty much sit in the apartment for three months, while I rode around Burbank in a car.

Widdup also believed in tracting, or door-to-door knocking. Never mind that tracting had proven to be woefully ineffective, and everyone knew it. Widdup thought that hours and hours of tracting proved to God that you were willing to sweat for The Work. I thought it was a huge waste of time, and a morale punch in the groin. Having doors slammed in your face all day does not make you feel good about what you are doing for two years in your prime. I started very early in my Mission considering how we could be more productive in finding and teaching people. Tracting was a century-long tradition, but I did not care. Bad strategy is bad strategy.

Through a member of the Ward to which Widdup and I were assigned, the Burbank 5th Ward (Spanish), we were given the name and address of the Perez family. The day we went over to their house, we got rear-ended at a stop light. We thought it was bad luck; but in retrospect, I know the Adversary did not want us to go over there.

We arrived and met the family: parents, Jorge and Maria, teenage sons Halbert (pronounced "all-bear"), Jorge Jr. (or "yoon-your"); pre-teen daughter, Brenda; and a 5-year-old son, Giovanni, who was my best friend for many, many months. My Spanish was still in its infancy, but they were kind and helpful.

Jorge worked in a factory making those Halliburton aluminum-shell briefcases. He gave me one that I sent to my Dad, who carried it for years. Jorge was a former "coyote"; someone who picks up undocumented immigrants from the U.S.-Mexico border, brings them into the country, forges their papers, and finds them work/housing. Yes, this is a very clinical view of *coyotes*, who were often criminally dishonest and murderous, but Jorge was one of the good ones…which was probably why he stopped doing it. His *coyote* connections would prove to be useful later.

Maria mostly stayed home, but she did some housecleaning for other families to bring in some extra money. She was my first experience with home cooking, Latino-style. If eating her food was the life blood of a Mission, I never wanted to go home. Their kids were fun, and they taught me the Chicano tradition of communication. The Perez kids would speak only in English to their parents, and their parents would speak only Spanish back to them. It was surreal.

Parents: Adónde van?
Kids: To the store.
Parents: Tráeme unos pan dulces.
Kids: Ok, but I need more money.
Parents: Ven, te doy más.
Kids: Thank you.
Parents: Ten cuidado.

Coyotes

Kids: Ok, love you.
Parents: Te quiero también mijo.

I once asked why one or the other didn't just speak the other's language, and they looked at me like I was nuts. That's just how they communicated; it never occurred to them to do so, though I always sensed a slight sadness on the side of the parents that their language and culture was being lost. In the same breath, however, they would tell you they wanted their kids to speak English, so they would have the same opportunities as everyone else in the United States.

After a few wonderful meetings with them, it came time to "commit" them. This is the process of inviting someone to be baptized and join The Church of Jesus Christ of Latter-day Saints. We explained baptism to them, and of course they volunteered that they had been baptized Catholic already. We explained priesthood authority, and that if they wanted "true" baptism, the ordinance had to be performed by someone holding the priesthood authority of God. This took some explaining; we walked them through Jesus Christ organizing His church during His mortal ministry; the Apostasy, or loss of the original church organization (being delicate about the role of Catholicism), to the Restoration of Christ's church and Priesthood by John the Baptist and Peter, James, and John to Joseph Smith and Oliver Cowdery in this dispensation, or era. We talked about how we both had been conferred that same priesthood.

The entire teaching process that Mormon missionaries facilitate has two parts. The first is teaching the principles of the doctrine of Jesus Christ directly from all revealed scripture. The second is challenging people, looking into the Church, to ask God for themselves, and allow the Holy Ghost to testify to them of the

 Priesthood Restoration

truthfulness of what they've learned. Once that process has been completed (both parts), and the people express a desire to be baptized, then the missionaries make all the necessary arrangements.

We could see their worry, as they suddenly considered the possibility that their baptism was not going to get them where they wanted to go after this life. We asked if they would be willing to pray with us to see if they were ready to be received unto baptism in the true Church of Jesus Christ on earth.

Jorge prayed first, and then Maria. Their prayers were sincere and heart-felt. Brenda asked to pray. In her prayer (in Spanish, of course), she said, "God…please help my parents get baptized. I want them to be in Heaven with me…and I'm getting baptized. Amen." It was the sweetest thing I had ever heard anyone say. We all got up off our knees and sat back down together. Maria just looked at Jorge with eyes that had hopeful-anguish in them. When he smiled and said, "let's do it" (also in Spanish), she broke down into tears of joy. Widdup and I just sat there as they all tearfully celebrated together. I had never been through that kind of faithful and immediate conversion, having been born in the Church. I didn't know what to feel.

The next week we returned to interview them, and do the baptism paperwork. Interviews had to be conducted by district leaders, but since Widdup was a District Leader, the Zone Leader, Elder Hansen came to do the interviews. Zone leaders usually have 4-5 districts in their zones, or 16-20 companionships, or 32-40 missionaries. It was my first-time meeting zone leaders, and they seemed so knowing and professional…like the NFL of missionaries.

When we all sat down together, the Perez family said they were struggling. Once their *familia católica* learned they were

Mission Organization and Overview

considering converting to Mormonism, their family had disowned them. Not because they had joined, but for just considering it; their friends and family had turned their backs on them. Little did I know it then, but this was a cultural phenomenon in the Latino community.

The late 80s were a turbulent time in Central America. Civil wars were being waged in nearly every country, with Guatemala, Nicaragua, and Honduras being the worst. People were fleeing on foot, through Mexico, all the way to the United States. The immigrant-refugees were coming with a mindset of leaving everything behind including their religion. Though the Catholic Church was pushing back against this in the Southern California communities, the proselytizing religions were having a field day….era. Between us, the Jehovah's Witnesses, and the Seventh-day Adventists, the competition was fierce. Some days it was dog-eat-dog, and other days it was the opposite.

The Perez family was feeling it.

Widdup asked how they wanted to proceed. After what seemed like an eternity of silence, Jorge said, "look, this is tough for us, which means it must really be important. If it was too easy, I guess I'd be worried. We know this is the true Church of Jesus Christ on earth. We want to be a part of it." I was stunned.

As they all took turns being interviewed, I sat quietly off to the side. I had a problem. Suddenly I could not stop thinking about my own testimony (level of belief) in The Church. I never really had to defend it. I mean, sure, being one of only two Mormons in my high school, I had my share of troubles among the Southern Baptists of East Texas, but I never had to defend my testimony to myself. I was pioneer-stock, meaning that my ancestors on my Mom's side were Day 1 members of the Church. We were Mormons, and this is just what we did. But now, sitting in a cramped apartment in Burbank, California, all of 19 years old, I could not erase or shake the thought that my testimony was not as strong as the new-to-the-Gospel Perez family was showing.

In fact, the more I sat there, the more I had the thought: "I'm not sure if I have a testimony at all…I'm not even sure I know what one feels like." I wanted to throw up, and I started sweating through my shirt. Maria had made some pozole, so when she asked if I was ok, because of the sweat showing on my face and through my shirt, I blamed it on the pozole being too hot. She laughed and said I would get used to it. Heading out to the MTC in Provo had nothing to do with knowing that Joseph Smith restored the true Church of Jesus Christ on the earth and that the Book of Mormon is scripture equal to the Bible. Only the Holy Ghost can testify of that, and at this point in my life, I doubted…or better yet, wondered if I really believed.

So that night, after companion study and prayer (both a part of a missionary's morning and evening routine), Widdup turned out the lights. After I heard him start to snore lightly, I slipped back out of my bed and onto my knees. I cannot adequately express the desperation in my prayer. I admired the Book of Mormon prophet Enos' confidence as he "wrestled" with the Lord. I pleaded: *You have to let me know that the Church is true. I cannot face going home. Staying here is my only option, and I cannot stay if I cannot believe.*

I just kept up my prayer in that vein for a very long time that night.

At one point, around midnight, I felt like I should read my scriptures. I grabbed my set and went into the bathroom, so as not to awake Widdup. I opened my scriptures to Alma 5:26 and read:

> And now behold, I say unto you, my brethren, if ye have experienced a change of heart, and if ye have felt to sing the song of redeeming love, I would ask, can ye feel so now?

I knelt in the bathroom, and as I started to pray, my mind raced with memories of times I had felt the Spirit in my life: Seminary with Sis May, Sunday School with Bro Cline, Priesthood classes with Bro Barber, meeting President Benson, and many others. The point was clear - you have felt the confirmation of the Holy Ghost in your life many times, so why can't you now? When I had that thought, I was suddenly filled with the Holy Spirit. The Lord communicated with precise clarity that I was loved, that He knew me, and that I was doing what I supposed to be doing at that time in my life.

Kneeling on a bathroom floor in Burbank, I finally understood the difference between the sweet purity of the Holy Spirit I was feeling, and the paralyzing darkness of the evil spirit I felt that night back in Texas, before my Mission began. I was quickly becoming something (or someone) else.

My next thought was, "Ok, but how is this all done? How in the world can I accomplish this enormous task of inviting people to *Come unto Christ*?" As I pondered this, I continued to read. The next four verses of Alma 5 gave me a road map that I would follow for the next two years, then jumping to verse 33.

> Have ye walked, keeping yourselves blameless before God? Could ye say, if ye were called to die at this time, within yourselves, that ye have been sufficiently humble? That your garments have been cleansed and made white through the blood of Christ, who will come to redeem his people from their sins?
>
> Behold, are ye stripped of pride? I say unto you, if ye are not ye are not prepared to meet God. Behold ye must prepare quickly; for the kingdom of heaven is soon at hand, and such an one hath not eternal life.
>
> Behold, I say, is there one among you who is not stripped of envy? I say unto you that such an one is not prepared; and I would that he should

prepare quickly, for the hour is close at hand, and he knoweth not when the time shall come; for such an one is not found guiltless.

Behold, he sendeth an invitation unto all men, for the arms of mercy are extended towards them, and he saith: Repent, and I will receive you.

Ok, I knew what I had to do.

The Perez Family was the first to be baptized on my Mission. It was a glorious day. I baptized Jorge and María and Widdup baptized the kids. It was the happiest moment in my life up to that point. Ok, I had had many happy moments, but it was through this experience I learned the difference between happiness and joy. If you've never considered the difference, I would describe it through a football analogy… of course.

There is no joy in being a Dallas Cowboys fan. Yes, I was happy when they won Super Bowls, but I'm more often mad as a bobcat in a suitcase as it pertains to "America's Team." One week-happy, next week-raging anger. There's no joy in being a Dallas Cowboys fan.

But, when it comes to my own children, it's nothing but joy. It lasts, it's eternal, it never disappoints. There's certainly anxiety around growth opportunities at every life-benchmark, but I cannot imagine life without them. The joy I feel to be their father is indefatigable and eternal.

The following year, I drove from Echo Park to the Los Angeles Temple on the day Jorge and María received their Endowments, and were Sealed for Eternity (eternal marriage) as a couple and as a family. Jorge would go on to serve in a Bishopric, and María was a Relief Society President for many years. All four of

[22] their children served missions. I only mention this because the retention rate in that area of the Church, at that time, was very low. Immigrant-refugees were indeed wanting to join an American religion, but they were still Catholics at heart. For many of them, it meant Christmas and Easter attendance. The Perez Family were stalwarts and devoted; never missing a Sunday.

I loved them.

Dales were beginning to evolve.

Elmer married Ella Frances Rusco, and they had many children including my grandfather Richard Benjamin Dale. He married Delores Elizabeth Baier, and after having three children on the "Dale Farm" south of Pratt, Kansas, they moved to Scott City on the western border near Colorado. I'm not sure what the religion the Dales had been historically, but Delores (my Grandma Dale), made them Catholic.

My Grandpa Dale became a middle school teacher and principal; the first Dale to not die a farmer. Grandma Dale was of German-immigrant descent, and a devout Catholic. The Dale Farm is still in the family.

Now five generations removed from the family farming tobacco in Virginia, my Father, Richard Henry Dale, became the first to graduate college.

Goooool!!!!!!!!!!!!!!!!

Never let sports get in the way of the Work of the Lord. The Work and sports can exist alongside each other in the same world. Three times during my Mission, sports would play a central role in a fun story. This was the first one:

I hit the ground in Arcadia right around the time of World Cup 1986. At the time I grew up in East Texas, there was no soccer in my high school or any other school around. I'm pretty sure that my first recollection of knowing about soccer at all came in May of '86 while serving in Burbank.

24

We were walking down the street going door to door (referred to as tracting) and house after house when Widdup expressed frustration at not being received well at doors when World Cup was on. It was especially bad when Mexico was playing, and they were good that year. It was a bad day when Mexico lost to West Germany on penalty kicks 4-1.

The Zone Leaders finally called to say that if a game was on, we should not be knocking on doors. It was causing problems all around Los Angeles. But...Widdup was determined, so we soldiered on, and it was rough. At best, we would get invited in to watch the game. That was a tough conundrum for me.

On the one hand, my appreciation for soccer was not going to happen for three more decades. At that time, I thought soccer was stupid and made no sense. It just looked like marbles rolling around on the floor. On the other hand, I would have whooped and hollered right along with the people to get out of tracting. I mean, what's the choice? A morale killing waste of time or pretending to be into a sport that made no sense to me.

Whoever invented tracting as a missionary did not sell the joke well enough, so the other missionaries thought he was serious. I say "he" because, in my experience, sister missionaries are far more mature and way smarter. There's no way tracting was invented by anyone other than over-zealous Elders.

At any rate, I learned first-hand the passion of *latinoamericanos* as it relates to World Cup. It is intense. Some knowledge of the game would have come in handy. I had no idea about any of it, other than the people I was called to serve, loved it.

I can see in my mind standing at a screen door and hearing Andrés Cantor yell gooooooooooooooooool.... gooooooooooooooooool.... gooooooooooooooool!
If you have never heard him, YouTube it. He is really something. Legend.

The fútbol experience was one of many cultural revelations serving in the Arcadia Mission. Growing up in New Mexico, I was peripherally familiar. Texas helped none to prepare me culturally. I was fascinated by all of it.

The fútbol, the music, the food, the machismo in the men, and especially the telenovelas. My time in Arcadia was during the reign of *Cristal*. The only TV phenomenon I can think to compare it to is *Dallas*. The difference is that instead of a weekly show over a five-six-month season, telenovelas played 5-6 nights a week for a year, then concluded. The year of *Cristal* was something.

The other show we had to plan around was *Sábado Gigante,* which was a variety show. Good entertainment and plenty of scantily clad women for whole-family viewing.

Andrés Cantor

My Father tried to attend Kansas State, but after a fateful encounter with some rich frat boys, he transferred to Fort Hays State. It was 1960 at KSU, and he was walking across a parking lot headed to the gym when a pack of rich students ("city boys") pulled up in a convertible. Instead of parking, they got out, and the driver flipped my Father the keys and a $5 bill. "Park this for me, would you, and don't scratch the paint."

My Dad beat him bloody.

First Miracle

Widdup and I received an assignment from the Bishop to track down and check on a family who had recently joined the Church. Over the years, there has been much concern regarding the retention rate of the newly baptized. In my opinion, one main cause for the low rate is likely due to the fact that we have a different definition of what it means to be "active." In other religions, if you live by the dietary rules and attend on Christmas Eve and Easter, you are active.

In the Church of Jesus Christ of Latter-day Saints, activity requires significantly more. If you asked an active member what it means to be active, they might say any combination of:

1. Attend every Sunday…and even if you are out of town; you find a service to attend wherever you're visiting.

2. Hold a calling (or volunteer job) in the Church and work at it diligently.

3. Accept a home teaching, now ministering assignment. This is a list of four to five families that you will look after in a

service-supportive way. It's a pretty cool aspect of the Church.

4. Be working toward, or have an active temple recommend. Anyone can attend a Sunday, Sacrament meeting service, but a member of at least a year, and one living the commandments, can only go into a Temple with a recommend signed by both a Bishop (local leader) and a Stake President (regional leader).

5. Be living the Word of Wisdom (no illegal drugs, cigarettes, or alcohol); the Law of Chastity (only sex with your spouse); and be a full tithe payer (10% of your income).

Being active in the Church is not easy for new people, and can take years for them to really understand that the demands of discipleship mean a complete cultural shift.

So, off we went to find this less-active family. After looking at several possible addresses, we found them. Finding someone, even those hiding from us, is not a bad thing. We just want to know how they are doing, and if we can be of service in any way.

The day we finally knocked on this family's door, we could hear a baby crying inside. It was that guttural sound that a baby makes when they have been at it a while…rhythmic, sad, and hoarse.

The father/husband answered, looking distraught. I cannot describe the look of relief when he saw us. We had no idea what the problem was, but by his look, they needed help. We entered the home to find his wife and infant son on the couch. *Abuelita* (grandma) was in the kitchen stirring something in a big pot that made the apartment smell great.

As we sat down, the father/husband said that their baby was sick, and they did not know why. He affirmed that they had been to the hospital, and had been given medicine to bring down the baby's fever, but it had had no effect. The baby would not stop crying.

Without us asking, the father asked us to give his son a blessing. A Priesthood Blessing involves a drop of consecrated olive oil on the scalp of the receiver. Then two holders of the Melchizedek or higher priesthood place their hands on the head of the same, and they pronounce a prayer or blessing of healing. Up to this point on my Mission, I had only seen it done a couple of times, and I had only done it once.

Of course, Widdup and I had the appropriate priesthood *authority* to do this, but we had been sniping at each other all day, and our partnership was less than harmonious. It is not acceptable to attempt a blessing of healing if the two performing the ordinance are not in harmony with each other.

This is probably a good time to talk priesthood offices. The Melchizedek Priesthood is the power to serve and act in the name of God on earth to bless the lives of others. A subset of the Melchizedek Priesthood, called the Aaronic Priesthood, is an introductory priesthood power to serve the temporal needs of Church members. Within those two priesthoods are offices: in the Aaronic Priesthood - Deacon, Teacher, Priest; and in the Melchizedek Priesthood - Elder, High Priest, Bishop, Patriarch, Apostle, and Prophet. As missionaries, we all held the office of Elder in the Melchizedek, or Higher Priesthood.

So, with that priesthood, Widdup and I had the authority to pronounce a healing blessing, but we were not in harmony with each other. We asked to be excused to pray. Going together into their bathroom, Widdup and I knelt down, and took turns offering prayers asking for forgiveness of the Lord and of each other. When we exited, I could feel the difference. We had asked God to bless our effort, and at that moment, I knew He would.

Before we gave the blessing, Widdup asked the Dad if they were attending Church. It is certainly possible they were going to another Ward with extended family. He said that they had stopped going, and that he had taken to drinking again. When he said that, I scanned the room for the first time. There were Coors cans everywhere. That was my Dad's brand, so I was familiar with the sight of empties.

Widdup told this father that we would be honored to bless his child. When we took the baby, I got my first look at him. He was red-faced and sweaty, but the worst was his eyes and nose were completely caked shut with dried mucus. He was crying/hyperventilating. It was shocking…especially to a 19-year-old who had never even held a baby before.

I anointed…meaning I did the drop of consecrated oil with a short prayer. Afterward, Widdup then joined me by placing his hands on the baby's head while I held the infant in my arms. When he began, the baby really went into a fit. Though barely a year old, he used both his little hands to try and remove Widdup's hands from his head. This move surprised us both. It was as though whatever, or whomever, was vexing this child did not want servants of God near him.

Widdup gave a blessing, first commanding the baby to be healed of all sickness, then commanding any evil spirits to depart. He closed with, "As long as your parents stay true to their covenants, you will never be seriously ill again in your life." My thoughts were "wow" and "cool" simultaneously. Using the Lord's priesthood in such a way, we had sealing power and a divine promise that if we pronounced it in righteousness, it would be done.

Interestingly, he screamed one last horrific wail when Widdup cast out evil spirits and breathed heavy, quick breaths through the rest of the prayer. When the blessing was over, the baby stopped crying. We gave him back to his Mom, who immediately began to nurse him, as he had not eaten in several days.

Thankfully, *Abuelta* brought out chilaquiles, and we ate with the family; engaging them in small talk between each grateful mouthful. In the course of eating and conversing, we completely forgot about the baby until I pointed out that he had pulled himself up next to the couch, so that he could reach and play with some of his toys. Within an hour of the blessing, he was smiling, giggling, and having fun with his toys. His eyes and nose completely cleared up. The fever was gone. He was completely healed in a short amount of time. Crazy thing is: it never occurred to me that the healing blessing might not work. When you're raised in the Church, you hear so many stories about the use of priesthood power that when it's your turn, it's just that…your turn.

For the next two Sundays, the family came to Church. The Dad said he had stopped drinking. They all looked amazing, relieved, and very happy.

Then the next Sunday, they were not at Church.

Two weeks later, we received a phone call from the Mom. In the background we heard the baby screaming. She said she needed a ride to the hospital, as her husband was passed out drunk.

Breaking several mission rules, we headed out after our 9:30pm curfew, picked them up in our car, and took them to the hospital. They were undocumented, so we had to take them to a medical unit in Alhambra…way out of our area. They got help there, but the baby did not get better.

The next day, we went back to their apartment and offered the same blessing with the same result. To my knowledge, the Dad stayed faithful after that.

Priesthood Blessings

In the summer prior to his Senior year, Dad went to work laying phone line for AT&T. He was assigned a route laying line along the newly completed Highway 40. He joined the team in Amarillo, and got as far as St. Johns, Arizona when he decided to catch a movie and relax. He was literally a Wichita Lineman.

Down near the front of the theater, he caught the eye of the recently crowned Ms. Apache County and runner-up Ms. Arizona. She was on her way to Brigham Young University, but couldn't run out of theater fast enough. Dad had been a track star in high school. It paid off. Shortly thereafter, they married.

My mother, Mary Inez Conant, would never go to BYU.

Feels Like the First Time

A sister in the Ward invited us to dinner in her home. She had a cute little daughter, but no husband. She was on her own and had very little, but she wanted to feed us dinner. So many people, during my time in Arcadia, would insist on giving food to us, even though they had little for themselves. It was remarkable, and unforgettable.

In this case, though, I would have happily taken a pass. She made pozole...a kind of soup with pork and hominy. It's red and rich and HOT. I had already experienced the digestive chaos that results from a robust pozole session; however, a rule that I will reiterate throughout my story here is, as a missionary, you eat what is put in front of you. Period.

About a dozen spoonfuls in and three glasses of horchata (a rice-based drink with lots of sugar), I spilled a little pozole on my tie. I did not notice it at first, but eventually I looked down to see the soup had eaten a hole in my tie.

Uh oh, this cannot be good.

The ride home was painful. The only thing drowning out my moaning was Widdup's laughter. He had been out almost two years, and his stomach was acclimated. Mine, not so much.

We got home, and my evening was explosive. In between trips to the toilet, I laid on my mattress, which rested on the floor - having no frame - with the fan up near my head on full. I really thought I might die.

Fortunately, it would be the last time I had trouble with the food.

 Foreigner

Baptisms in Burbank 5th

Date	Name of Person	Baptized by:
11 May 86	Jorge Perez Perez	me
11 May 86	Maria de la Luz Perez	me
11 May 86	Halbert Perez Perez	Widdup
11 May 86	Jorge Perez Perez Jr	Widdup
11 May 86	Brenda Perez Perez	Widdup
18 May 86	Ariseli Beltran	Widdup
22 Jun 86	Yolanda Margarita Martinez	Widdup
20 Jul 86	Rigoberto Dardon Rivas	me
20 Jul 86	Maria Estela Sandoval	me
27 Jul 86	Gilda Godoyo Bustamante	Bustamante
3 Aug 86	Nelsa Caridad Villalunga	Hno Soliz
17 Aug 86	Victor Espinosa	Figueroa
17 Aug 86	Liliana Duarte	Figueroa
17 Aug 86	Esther Duarte	Figueroa

Everyone Widdup and I baptized the night before I left Burbank.

35

Yolanda Martinez

Victor, Liliana, and Ester Duarte

María Sándoval and Rigo Rivas

> Mary Farren Harrison first heard the Restored Gospel of Jesus Christ from Heber C. Kimball and Joseph Fielding in Vauxhall Chapel on July 23, 1837. The following Sunday, she was one of the original nine people to be baptized, who raced from Vauxhall Chapel down Avenham Lane to the trail off Ribbledale Road through Avenham Park to River Ribble that runs through the town of Preston, England.
>
> Her husband, William Rogerson, did not embrace the new American religion.

Into the Fire

After three months with Elder Widdup, I got the phone call saying that I was being transferred to North Hollywood, just a few miles away.

Transfer day is an exciting time for every missionary. It's like Christmas morning, in terms of anticipation. New area, new companion, new Ward, new people to teach…maybe increased responsibilities. It's a feeling that stays with you for the rest of your life; anytime you think about transfers.

The transfer call came from the Zone Leader, Elder Hansen: "pack your bags." Our guess was Widdup was leaving as he had been there longer. We thought they'd leave me in Burbank one more month to introduce a new Elder to the area. "White washing," or moving both missionaries, was rare. You always want one missionary in the pair who knows the people and the area. So, the move was a bit of a surprise.

What's more surprising is that the transfer to North Hollywood was also a *white wash*. Apparently both elders in the area had to be moved due to some inappropriateness going on with some member girls in the Ward there. When Widdup heard it was a *white wash*, and that I was going to the North Hollywood 4th Ward, he cautioned me to be careful…"watch out for those 4th Ward girls," he said.

My new companion was Elder Thomas Branham. He had only been in the Mission a month less than me, so we were both relatively new. His trainer, Elder Bolton, was a legend in the Mission. He was a champion "Bible basher," and young evangelical Christians all over Southern California would seek him out to argue scripture. Bolton had taught himself Greek and Latin, so he could argue Biblical interpretations from the Septuagint and Volgate in their original languages.

Branham, now my companion, missed Bolton, but he was glad at the possibility of doing some real work; not just carrying Bolton's books around like some kind of medieval squire. What Branham introduced me to, though, was books. He already had quite a collection, and we immediately started buying church books on theology and doctrine by the best authors: McConkie, Nibley, Sperry, Barker…we were spending all of our discretionary money on books. Our companionship study was really something. On the one hand, I was opened to a whole new world doctrinally. On the other, it didn't  make me a better missionary. I'm still an active collector of LDS church books thanks to Branham…and I suppose, thanks to Bolton.

When we got settled in, we hit the pavement. Now I'm riding a bike, so that was new and enjoyable. Only one month senior, but the Senior Companion nonetheless, I announced to Branham that we would not be doing any stupid tracting. My days of knocking doors were over…well, mostly. I still knocked a door here and there, but never hour after hour for days on end. The problem was, in those days, that's pretty much all missionaries did, so we had to ask ourselves - if we don't knock doors, how do we find people to teach?

In those days, every area had a Mission book that contained information of people contacted, people being taught, a Styrofoam based map of the area with pins showing where members lived, and a Thomas Guide (spiral-bound book of maps). We looked at the teaching pool and discovered a healthy list of 10-15 names. We set out to contact those folks, only to find out they had either moved, or had no further interest…one person on the list had died. Next, we went to the Ward Mission Leader, who told us that not much of anything was going on.

That first week in North Hollywood was a rude awakening. We had nothing.

We rode solemnly to our first Sunday meeting in the Ward. In every Sacrament meeting there's always room to sit in the middle toward the front. We saw an opening, and we took our seats. We arrived right before the beginning of the meeting, so there had been no chance to meet people. As we sat down, I could feel the curiosity following us to our seats. We were the only missionaries assigned to the Ward at that time, which was unusual for an area like North Hollywood, but the missionaries had had such a hard time there with nonsense issues that the Mission President had moved everyone out. Branham and I could feel the pressure of the situation.

After the one-hour Sacrament meeting ended with a prayer, the organ postlude launched, and just as I started to stand, I felt a tap on my shoulder. Turning around, I was greeted by two women in their late 50s or early 60s. One of the sisters said, "Hello Elders, I'm Sister Sandovál, the Bishops' wife, and this is my sister-in-law, Carmen. She has something to tell you."

Carmen, already weeping, said that she was not a member of the Church, though she had a deep devotion to the Gospel. She said that many years prior, while being taught by the missionaries, she had had a dream about being baptized. The missionary baptizing her did not look like either of the Elders teaching her at the time. She woke up from the dream knowing she had to wait for that Elder to come teach and baptize her. Putting her finger in the middle of my chest she said, "It's you Elder. You're the missionary I saw in my dream many years ago. I'm ready to be baptized now." My Spanish was not yet at an expert level, but I understood every word.

Stunned, I did not know what to say. I just stared at her with my mouth hanging open. By this time, the Bishop had come down from the stand, and his wife quickly recounted to him what his sister had just said to me. Without warning he embraced me tearfully, thanking me for coming to North Hollywood. I think about his comment often, wondering what in the world would have happened to Carmen had I not served a Mission. We baptized her the following Sunday.

The news of Carmen's baptism mesmerized the Ward. They all knew the story; she had been telling it for years, as well as apologizing to every set of missionaries who came through with the wrong face from her dream. The members were fascinated by me, treating me like the celebrity from Carmen's baptismal dream. Members started inviting us over to their homes in bulk. In a moment of inspiration,  our answer was, "We would love to come over for dinner, and please invite friends." We said this in the spirit of "the more the merrier, right?" Let's party! The Ward loved it.

We ate in homes all over the Ward, and met really great people. We would just talk to them, not preach. Our whole posture was,

"Let's be friends!" Eventually, our new friends would invite us to eat in their homes without the member/neighbor present. We would strike up conversations about religion, and they would ask questions. If it evolved into an official missionary discussion, we would always end with," So, how does knowing this story make you feel?" If they responded positively, we would make a return appointment then ask," Hey, would you mind introducing us to the people across the street? We just want to meet them." About every other time it happened, that new family would invite us in to talk. We would always invite the person we had just taught to sit in with us, and so on. On a couple of occasions, we ended up at the end of the street with a dozen people in a house, teaching about the Restored Gospel. It was crazy effective. We were changing culture, not just hunting people to teach.

There's a street in North Hollywood named Strathern. It's between Vineland and the 5 freeway. We taught everyone on that street and baptized most of them.

As a daily act of service, Branham would make my bed when I took my shower in the morning.

"The Saints," or members of the Church of Jesus Christ of Latter-day Saints, arrived in the Salt Lake Valley on July 24, 1847, just over three years after the death of the Prophet Joseph Smith. They arrived by wagon, by foot, and by horseback from the marshaling community they named Winter Quarters, Nebraska. Two years later, the new Prophet and President of the Church, Brigham Young, announced the creation of the Perpetual Emigration Fund, which provided money for the European convert's travel expenses if they chose to come to "Zion" in the Salt Lake Valley.

"The Call to Zion" sounded across the Atlantic, and Mary Farren Harrison announced her intention to go.

The Hooker

Branham and I taught a woman named Lupe. I'll spare you her real name for a reason. When we met her, she asked us not to come over to teach her until her "husband" left the house in the morning. That was in the days prior to "ratios." Today, missionaries cannot teach or be alone with members of the opposite sex without an equal number of missionaries, or members, of the same sex as the person being taught. If that's not clear: two Elders teaching a single woman, alone, would not be allowed today…and for good reason.

In my missionary era, we were cautioned, but there was no rule or restriction. So, we would wait until the tan-colored Impala turned the corner, before pedaling up to the small house to teach Lupe and her two children ages five and seven.

She was really getting serious about the Gospel when she

decided to tell us more about her life. The man she lived with was not her husband, but her pimp. She was a prostitute, and the two children were his, but she was clear that the sex was not consensual. It was horrific. We were too young and naive to handle what she was saying to us. I certainly had no experience with this coming from rural East Texas. As we rode away that day, all we could do was look at each other and ask, "What the heck are we going to do?"

Back in our apartment we consulted with the English language missionaries, or "Anglos," Elders Jones and Mast. Funny thing: they were knuckleheads - so consulting with them was like asking a couple of circus clowns for directions to the hospital. Branham and I were at a loss. And for the record, Branham was as hillbilly as I was or more! The next morning over cereal and McConkie, Branham asked me, "If you could do anything to help Lupe, regardless of mission rules, or money, or the law; what would you do?" Now he's speaking my language…I thought for a second and responded: "I would get her out of there!" He raised one eyebrow, and smiled a wry-smile. We were going to get her out of there. Cue the banjos…

We decided to rent a U-Haul, and get all the missionaries in the Zone to help us. I called up my first baptism, Jorge Perez from Burbank and asked if he could get us a driver's license and three social security cards.

"No problem," which sounded like, "No pro-lem."

A prominent member of the North Hollywood 4th Ward was part owner and manager at a textile factory in San Fernando, so we had a job lined up for Lupe. The women's leader, Relief Society President, helped us find an apartment for Lupe in San Fernando. It was outside of our area, and leaving the area was against mission rules; we did not care. I was quickly developing a willingness to break mission boundary rules to get the job done. We referred to it as "a strategem" (a Book of Mormon term for winning outside the box) and not disobedience. We found the bus routes from the new apartment in San Fernando to the textile mill, and from the apartment to the elementary school where we enrolled Lupe's kids using their new Social Security cards. The stage was set.

Oh wait, Lupe wanted to be baptized and join the Church.

She was still in the pimp's house while we set up a new life for her. It took us a couple of weeks to get it all done. In the meantime, we had continued to teach her the Gospel. The day came for her baptismal interview, and the District Leader, Elder Beutler, met us at the house. Branham and I sat outside, playing with her kids, while Lupe was being interviewed...which usually only lasted ten to fifteen minutes. After a half an hour, I started to look over at the front door like, "What is going on in there."

Pretty soon the District Leader emerged looking ashen. Apparently, Lupe had decided to confess every pregnancy and every abortion she had ever had. She talked about her life as a prostitute and every bad experience she had ever had. The poor 20-year-old missionary was not equipped to hear all that. None of us were. We grew up fast that day, and many others after it. A follow up interview with the local, regional leader, or Stake President and she was ready for baptism.

There's a huge difference in baptizing an 8-year-old and baptizing a prostitute in her late 20s, early 30s. Both baptisms have the same force and effect, but I tell you... baptizing Lupe...you really felt like a lot of cleansing was going on. She had many a reason to be baptized. The joy she exhibited, after being cleansed of all sins, is indescribable.

Now baptized, it was time to get her out of the pimp's house she was in. We wasted no time. A missionary's day off is Monday, so baptism on Saturday (she told the Pimp she was going to stay with her sister in East L.A.), then stay the night with the Bishop and his family, confirmation Sunday, then again with the Bishop's family before the move on Monday.

All of the missionaries in the Zone came to our apartment, and we loaded everyone's bikes in the back of the biggest U-Haul we could find. A member of the 4th Ward rented it for us, and drove it over to the pimp's house with all 20-plus missionaries in the back with our bikes. We waited around the corner until the tan Impala left, sped up to the house, piled out with our bikes, threw them in the yard, and went to work.

We unloaded the entire house in short order. We took everything. The home was so disgusting and gross. There were roaches and rodents everywhere. Having prepared ahead of time, we were ready with bug bombs that we placed along the back of the truck. We set them off, then quickly shut the big U-Haul truck door. We were on the road in under two hours billowing bug spray smoke out of the back of the truck.

Lupe had a new life, inside and out. The problem with moving her: she was now in a new Ward. We never saw her again, though we would hear about her from time to time. She was doing great, staying active in her San Fernando Ward.

On the other hand, The Pimp did not take it well. Later in the week of her escape, we were riding our bikes west-bound on Saticoy about a block or two from Vineland. Branham, in front of me, was riding fast as usual. A state champion wrestler from South Carolina; he was compact and strong. I was neither of those things, but athletic enough to keep up.

As we rode along, I remember hearing horns and brakes and engines revving. Not thinking anything of it, I looked over my shoulder to see the pimp's Impala coming up fast behind us. I continued to look as the car got right next to us. Frankly, even as the car pulled up next to me, I still had not processed that it was The Pimp…until I saw the shotgun.

He laid it across the open passenger window. I saw the barrel plain as day. Hitting the brakes, I yelled, "Branham, gun!" Just then, The Pimp pulled the trigger blowing out the window of a parked car right in front of me. Branham was on alert, but also still processing when the shotgun blast caused him to dive off his bike into some bushes on the side of the street. I had jumped off my bike also and sought cover behind a parked car.

The Pimp, having missed us both, sped away. I mean, it was a busy street…though no one stopped. We jumped back up, grabbed our bikes and rode back to our apartment on the corner of Vineland and Saticoy.

Once inside, we jumped around and yelled, "Holy crap!" over and over for several minutes. What do we do? Call the police? No, the entire story was not a good look for us or the Church. We had kinda/sorta robbed that guy and had obtained falsified documents for an undocumented immigrant and her two kids. There were many moving parts involving a lot of people.

Do we call the Mission President, Zone Leaders, or District Leaders? That was the "right" thing to do, but again we had broken I don't know how many mission rules, so not a good look for us. Reporting that we were shot at would have caused the Mission to transfer both of us immediately, and we now had a ton of good people we were teaching at the time; neither one of us wanted to give them up. And that meant the Mission would have to *white wash* the poor 4th Ward again, and we had fallen in love with the people and the area. So, we would keep it to ourselves.

We did decide to tell Jones and Mast, so they would be careful in case The Pimp found out where we lived. For the next several months, we took different routes to and from the apartment and church, and we stayed way away from the pimp's street.

46 We never saw The Pimp again, but it wasn't the last time our lives would be threatened in North Hollywood.

William Rogerson would not be going to America.

He did not accept the message of the Restored Gospel of Jesus Christ. He supported his wife, and nine of their eleven children had followed "Mother" in baptism.

On the appointed day in 1856, William travelled with Mary and the children to Liverpool where they would board the ship *Horizon* for the journey to America. He was certainly hoping she would change her mind. As Mary exited the wagon, and headed to the ship's entrance, the two had their final exchange. William spoke first, "You're tearin' the very heart out of me, Mary."

"It's me life, William; it's me life." She turned and ascended the stairs without her husband.

The Ranger

After knocking on the door of a contact we received who did not answer, we were descending the staircase in an apartment complex near Laurel Canyon and Keswick. As we reached the bottom of the stairs, a very attractive woman carrying a young boy passed us going up. She smiled at us and said, "Hello." When we said "Hola hermana" in return, she stopped and asked why we spoke Spanish.

We told her we were missionaries for The Church of Jesus Christ of Latter-day Saints, and would she like to hear a message regarding His Restored Gospel? She said that she would, but asked if we could come back later. We made

an appointment to return the next day.

We came back the next day not expecting her to be there. We thought the appointment was a brush off, but we knocked anyway. Nancy Zelaya greeted us warmly and invited us inside her nicely furnished apartment. The place smelled of food cooking, and she invited us to sit and eat a meal of carne asada, arroz y frijoles. She had made the tortillas herself, and the salsa made me want to sing *Volver Volver*. She liked Branham and me from the start and called us "gauchos," or "cowboys." It was fair; East Texas and South Carolina had come calling.

In short order, we taught Nancy the missionary lessons, and she was ready to be baptized. About half way through the lessons, she shared with us a worry that her husband, Miguel, may not support her joining the Church. We had not seen or heard anything about a husband, so immediately we were worried. This was a surprise, and missionaries do not like surprises; though they happen in almost every case of someone joining the Church. We asked her how she wanted to proceed, and she said that it was her desire to be baptized; however, when her husband returned from his deployment, it would be tense for a while.

What's a deployment? These were pre-military years for me, so I had no idea what that was or that it even pertained to the military at all. So, we were both surprised when she said he was an Army Ranger away on a six-month assignment. Great, a Ranger. We were scared of The Pimp, but he was a pimp; not a trained killer. A Ranger could dispose of us and just make up an alibi. So, at the same time we were setting up Maria's life in San Fernando, we were now trying to navigate dangerous waters with Nancy.

Volver, Volver

Nancy was baptized on a Sunday, and the following day, her husband Miguel came home. We were unaware of his arrival as we stopped by to check on Nancy and celebrate her baptism. When we entered the apartment, Miguel greeted us warmly. Ok, he was huge…with a body builder frame and a handsome face. His smile put us right at ease. We had a nice conversation over some amazing flán. He did not even mention the Church, nor did he ask us any questions about the Gospel, or what we were doing as missionaries. The hair on my neck did stand, though, when he asked where we lived. Before I could lie about it, Branham said, "Arcadia." "Wow," I thought, "that's far for bikes"…dang it.

After a nice evening with their family, we excused ourselves and left. We descended the stairs three at a time, but as we unlocked our bikes, I became aware that Miguel was right behind us. I didn't even hear him coming. He must have enjoyed my slightly perceptible jump and that I almost crapped myself. Without a word, he held out his hand, fist clenched and palm down, as though he had something hidden in his hand that he wanted to give me. I held out my hand, palm up, and he deposited a huge bullet in my hand. I looked at it, then at him. "If I ever see either of you again," he growled, "I'll put this in your skull, not your hand." He turned with an ease that made the threat even more menacing. We rode home as fast as we could taking turns looking back over our shoulders.

Again, it was pre-Army, but within a year after returning home I would learn at Ft. Leonard Wood that the bullet was a 7.62 round commonly fired from an M-60 machine gun. Those bullets were meant to pierce armor, not humans; though people are a frequent target of 7.62 rounds. Funny end to the bullet: I kept it, and took it back to Texas after my Mission.

At that time, Bishop Sandovál was on a kick that the Ward needed to sit in the center rows of the Chapel. You see, most LDS chapels have three banks of pews. One set of wide rows in the center with two narrow sets of rows on either side. Bishop

Sandovál felt like the Ward lacked unity, so one way to create a closer-knit family was to have everyone sit closer together. He asked us missionaries to sit in the narrow rows on each side and act as ushers. If people came in late, we could direct them to the center. So, as a result, we could be found each Sunday sitting on the sides of the Chapel by ourselves. Out in the open. Exposed.

When my new companion arrived after Branham, the unity project was still going on. On a Sunday in December, just after the opening hymn began, I looked up to see Miguel standing in the aisle next to the row where I was sitting. I almost screamed out like a pre-teen walking through a Haunted House. My new companion was clueless as to what was happening, and he was seated alone in the small bank of pews on the other side of the Chapel.

Immediately, I missed Branham, who had once wondered out loud to me as to whether I thought he could "take Miguel." Frankly, I would have given money to see them fight. They were both tough dudes. Nonetheless, Miguel got the drop on me, so I was at his mercy.

After looking down at me for what seemed like an eternity, he slid into the pew, and sat really close to me. I'm already sweating through my shirt, but I took a deep breath and offered the left-hand corner of the hymnal for him to grab and join in the singing. To my surprise, he did. Although he did not know the hymn, he had a beautiful singing voice, and did his best to follow along.

After the prayer, we both just continued to sit there looking forward…neither saying anything nor making a move. I wanted to stand up and yell, "HELP!" but I somehow held it together. I could not see my new companion's face, but a quick look let me know he had not even taken notice of my predicament. I had not told him the story of Nancy or the M-60 round. I just sat there rubbing the palms of my hands back and forth on my pants as if to keep them dry. Miguel made no indication that he noticed anything I was doing or feeling. Neither of us moved a muscle for the entire hour-long meeting.

Head and eyes to the front, soldiers!

When the meeting ended, Miguel did not move. Members of the Ward filed passed us, and some even attempted to greet us. I simply smiled and nodded them away. Miguel acknowledged no one. After the Chapel was empty, we still sat there. Finally, after a long silence, he stood, turned, looked down at me and said, "I cannot fight my wife on this. I liked the service. Baptize me…now."

We filled the font and baptized him that evening. My smile in the photo should be interpreted as, "Holy crap, I'm not dead!"

Army Rangers

By 1856, the Saints crossing the American Continent to the Salt Lake Valley did so by walking and pulling handcarts containing their belongings. Ten total groups or 16,000 converts of handcart pioneers travelled the 1,300 miles from Iowa to the Utah Territory. The Saints, including my great-great-great grandmother, Mary, who was aboard the *Horizon* arrived at Winter Quarters, Nebraska, late in the season. After a legendary meeting, it was determined the Martin Handcart Company would go to Salt Lake anyway, ignoring the winter weather warnings. The fatal journey would result in twenty-five percent of the company dying along the trail. Though all of her children survived, only six would complete the journey.

For her part, Mary lost all her toes from frostbite, and her hands would never again straighten from grasping the crossbar of the handcart. She settled in Parowan, Utah where she opened a laundry service.
She died, and was buried there in 1888.

The Pastor

Every Sunday, Branham and I rode our bikes the length of Saticoy from our apartment on Vineland to the Stake Center. It's an adventure to ride a bike in L.A., and we always had one eye out for danger. Riding one day, I got hit in the head with a beer bottle, and another time a truck brushed Branham's shoulder with their side mirror. We got cussed at on the regular, and people would honk and yell all manner of threats.

Our route home from the Stake Center passed in front of a church that is still there named Iglesia Fuente de Vida, or Source of Life Church. It is an evangelical Christian church, and on some days, we could hear raucous singing going on inside.

They had a full rock band, including a massive organ that could be heard for blocks.

On days when their church was letting out as we passed, we would get off and walk our bikes through their exiting crowd. We did it to be polite, but over time people would start to greet us. The courteous kindness quickly turned into conversations, and before we knew it, we were getting dinner and teaching appointments.

One Sunday, as we passed through the crowd greeting people by name, the Pastor intercepted us and inquired who we were and what we were doing. We told him who we were and simply said that we were headed home after our church service. The Pastor remarked that he thought our chapel was beautiful, and that he knew and liked Bishop Sandovál.

To our surprise, he ended the conversation by asking if we would like to preach to his congregation. Branham and I looked at each other and then eagerly accepted. Preaching in another church is some 1840's, Heber C. Kimball stuff right there (Google it) so, we were feeling pretty lofty as we rode home.

We called Bishop Sandovál to let him know we would not be in Church the following Sunday and asked if he had any advice. "Yes," he said, "our organist is moving. Steal theirs." We thought he was kidding, but he wasn't. We laughed after hanging up, thinking that if we managed to get out of there alive, it would be enough. I mean, we had survived Miguel and The Pimp, so how hard could this be?

The following Sunday, we sat behind the pulpit with the Pastor and rocked out with the congregation, clapping and singing like I was back visiting the Southern Baptist Church on the black side of town with my good friend, John Starling. Seriously, we

Heber C Kimball and early church missionaries

both must have looked like Forrest Gump up there with the Greenbow Baptist Church choir.

Our time came to speak, and The Pastor introduced us to an impressive round of applause, which was new for us. Mormons don't applaud in chapel meetings, but I remember thinking I could get used to it if the rule ever changed. It was kinda nice. I almost raised my hands in victory, like the motion boxers make after they are declared the winner…but I refrained.

Not knowing what subject to cover, we decided to just deliver the first and second missionary discussions. We covered our belief in God, Jesus Christ, modern-day prophets, modern-day scripture, and the concepts of faith, repentance, baptism, and the gift of the Holy Ghost. They were attentive and kept raising their hands, rocking back and forth, and "mhmm"-ing when we would make a point they liked. I also liked the live feedback.

It really amped us up, and by the end, we must have looked like street preachers down on Sunset.

My final comment, after testifying of Jesus Christ, was, "oh, and if you play piano or organ, talk to me after." As we shook every hand in the place, Alma Trinidad Mendoza del Rosario Gutierrez whispered that she played the organ. We asked if we could come over to her house with a request, and she agreed. Three weeks later we baptized her, and she became the North Hollywood 4th Ward organist immediately…in fact, she started playing the organ in Sacrament meeting two weeks prior, but officially the Sunday after her baptism.

I'm not sure how long she served as the organist, but missionaries would later report to me that she was still at the North Hollywood Stake Center, rocking the house…LDS-style.

Mary's youngest son, John Edward, was only 9-years-old. The policy of the handcart leadership was to take the shoes of children under fourteen. Without socks, leather shoes were causing more problems to the children's feet than they were worth, and the bare feet would be "as tough as shoe leather by the first crossing of the Platt."

Unless it snowed.

Mary told John to take a wash tub and a blanket, run to the front of the two-mile long handcart train, get in the wash tub, cover his feet with the flannel blanket until the last handcart passed, then get up and run to the front, and repeat…or 1,300 miles. A 9-year-old.

Not sure how many 9-year-olds you know, but my great-great grandfather, John Edward Rogerson, had big-league patience. He made it all the way to Salt Lake without any frostbite.

The Wolves

Getting yelled at, knowing how to react to it, and knowing how to cope with it is all part of being a missionary for The Church of Jesus Christ of Latter-day Saints. Some of those who aren't yelling, don't trust the missionaries. In Arcadia, many of the people in the Latino community thought we were government agents…or at the least… government informants. We were called immigration (la migra) or CIA (la see-uh) or DEA (la day-uh) all the time.

Bottom line: we had to have thick skin on the outside and honest souls on the inside.

DEA and CIA

Riding north from our apartment on Vineland was the second most common route for Branham and me in North Hollywood. The grocery store and the laundromat were that way, and the little "nook" community of streets right under the 5-freeway was our fertile ground for teaching. We rode it so much, that a pit bull waited for us every day and menacingly barked while running alongside just on the other side of a fence that I prayed never gave way. If not, any missionary worth their salt could grab the Kryptonite lock from the frame between their legs and swing it like a cavalry officer at anything that might be attacking…two or four legs.

One day as we rode by, on guard from "Cujo" (our name for the dog), we noticed a flatbed trailer in front of the grocery store on the corner of Strathern and Vineland. What made it noticeable was the preacher yelling through a P.A. to a crowd that had gathered. He had a full band up there with him as he preached an apocalyptic version of Christianity full of warnings and admonitions to repent immediately or risk an eternity of hellfire and damnation. Street preachers are not unusual in SoCal, so we just gave the whole thing a passing curiosity.

As we rode by on the other side of the street, I heard him yell, "And my brothers and sisters, beware of wolves in sheep's clothing. Like those two wolves right there!" I looked, and he was pointing at us. Something about it just hit me wrong…maybe because it was in English, and my tolerance for abuse was limited to Spanish.

In front of Branham, I hit the brakes and crossed the street. He followed. I rode straight to the stage and jumped off my bike. The crowd became very quiet, and the man on the mic was equally shocked. Dumping my bike next to some make-shift stairs, I bounded up onto the stage with Branham in close pursuit.

The man on the mic identified himself as Esaias, and I introduced myself and Branham. He asked what we taught, and

I leaned into the microphone, "The True Gospel of Jesus Christ." Not much finesse there, but I was taught at an early age two rules: hit first and hit hard, and never bring a knife to a gunfight.

The preacher asked what made me think it was true, and I said that I didn't think it was true…I knew it was by the power of the Holy Ghost. He said that that was impossible, that we preached from a different Bible, so how could we claim such a thing?

I said that we also believed in the Bible and Jesus Christ, and that if I could show him something in the Bible that he couldn't explain, would he come to Church with us? He laughed mockingly in my face in a way that made me want to go into some hillbilly "laying on of hands," but to my astonishment he agreed to my challenge.

I asked him to read Genesis 2:24, which he did: "Therefore shall a man leave his father and his mother, and shall cleave unto his wife: and they shall be one flesh."

He read the verse and looked up at me with an attitude of "yeah, so?" I asked him who was speaking. He looked back down, then up and said, "Adam." I smiled and told him he was right. Before he could celebrate his victory, I asked him, "Who was Adam's mother?" He looked back down and realized he had been caught in a trap. I expected some lame interpretation, but to my surprise he simply said, "I don't know."

I turned to the crowd, nudging him completely away from the microphone, and said, "no one on this earth knows everything. We are all doing the best we can. My advice to all of you is find the truth that builds your faith, not tears it down. Sometimes I think we're all wolves trying to shed our skin and put on the repentant sheep's cloak."

We walked off. Some clapped, some thanked us, some walked away. By the time we got back on to Vineland, the band had struck up a guitar-laden number praising Jesus. Nothing ever

⁵⁸ came of that encounter that we know of. That guy never came to Church with us. To this day I imagine someone in that crowd answering their door at home, seeing two missionaries, remembering what they saw that day, and letting them in to have a discussion. That would make the exchange worth it. Otherwise, it's a good story, but not worth much else.

> After enduring epic hardship, great-great-great grandmother, Mary, walked into the Salt Lake Valley with six of her children. One daughter peeled off in Wyoming. Two daughters left the party near Devil's Tower with the "Mountain Men" trackers who traded supplies for women. I pray that the blood of Mary's strength and independence courses through the veins of my daughters.
>
> Her youngest son, John Edward, would marry Sarah Jane Perkins, and they would be one of the first five families to settle Monticello, Utah, on assignment from Brigham Young.

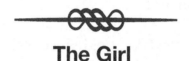

The Girl

Prior to my Mission, I was active socially. Going out to a dance club or taking a girl on a date was a regular occurrence. Once I hit the mission field, my focus was completely on The Work. My interest in girls, or dating, was definitely on hold. I was there to do a job.

I didn't even really think about it.

One Sunday in the 4th Ward, we were assigned to teach the Sunday School class. These classes are usually taught by the local members in the Ward, but it is not unusual to default to the full-time missionaries if the teacher does not show up for Church that day.

On this day, we were asked to teach the lesson. Members often think that missionaries are primed to teach at a moment's notice, but that is not true. They need to prepare just like anyone else, but it never happens that way. We got asked just minutes before class was to start.

So, I was up teaching…in Spanish…when I noticed a girl on the second row. She looked to be in her mid-20s, and she was stunning. Elder Branham and I had been in the Ward for about six weeks, and I had never seen her before. She was actively participating in the class, and it never occurred to me that she was flirting. On the way back to our apartment, Branham started in on me about how hard she was working on me. I had no idea, which was unusual for me, being serially flirtatious in my life up to that point.

The next Sunday she was back again. When I saw her, she took my breath away. She had eyes the size of moons, and her smile lit up the room. I loved her laugh. She was tall and shapely, and I was stricken. It was scary.

I was not in Arcadia for that.

Now, it wasn't like we didn't get female attention. Missionaries get that attention everywhere. Normally you just brush it off. There's something about the boyish, clean-cut look of an LDS full-time missionary that draws a lot of attention. To make matters worse, we had been told (seriously, we had been told) that right around the time I came to the mission field (early 1986) Playboy had released a list of the most wanted…or most desired…most lusted after men in the world. Mormon missionaries were number 1 with the explanation of being baby-faced, clean-cut virgins who needed to be de-flowered, and apparently that drove girls nuts. We got whistled at, propositioned, and cat-called frequently. We just smiled and waved back.

No big deal. Life as an international sex symbol is just part of the gig, right?

Well, here it was happening to me in a very real way. Was it unusual for a missionary to find his/her wife on the Mission? No. I never really understood the mechanics of how that could happen and still keep mission rules, but I knew it happened. I suppose it is important to mention that during the time of a full-time Mission, those who serve shun everything in the world…TV, music, movies, non-religious literature, dating, partying…everything that has nothing to do with serving. That said: I know plenty of faithful, active LDS people who met their spouse "legally" while serving their full-time Mission.

Olivia really liked me, and I really liked her. She would sit with Branham and me during Church, and she smelled great.

I was smitten.

At some point after a month of this Sunday flirting, I had decided to ask her if she would wait for me to complete my Mission, so we could date afterward. I got all dolled up in my best suit and tie to make the innocent proposal one Sunday morning. We arrived at Church, but no Olivia. Bishop Sandovál indicated that she had moved to Houston.

On the one hand, I had no idea she was going to move. On the other, I was from Houston, so I determined to find her when I returned home. A year and a half later, I did in fact find her. Apparently, she had moved to Houston to be closer to her parents, who could help with her little girl. She had become pregnant in North Hollywood and went back home to her parents. I met with her at her parent's house one day in the summer of 1988, met her daughter, and had a nice conversation…a really good day.

She asked if I had had feelings for her back in North Hollywood, and I admitted that I did. She indicated that she had feelings for me too, but had made a huge mistake in sleeping with this man she had met resulting in the pregnancy. I assured her that it was not a huge mistake; she had a beautiful daughter, and that was something important. She tearfully agreed, and gave me a big hug. It was the first time we had touched, other than shaking hands at Church, and it felt wonderful.

We talked again on the phone a time or two, and it became clear to both of us that I was not in a place to have a family. She needed a man who could be on her level at that point in her life, and I was not him. That was hard to admit and hard to hear, but it was the right decision for both of us.

I thought about her a lot for years, but eventually the memories faded. It was the one and only time that happened on my Mission, and I have never talked about it until now. It feels good to tell the story, because she deserves to be remembered. Even as I write, I can see her face and remember how it felt to be 19 and silly in love. It was pretty great, and I'm thankful to have known her. I have no idea where she is now; those few phone calls after my Mission in the summer of 1988 were the last contact we would ever have. My hope and prayer is that she is doing well…happy.

No matter how much love we find, there's always broken pieces inside us that contain fragments of feelings from the past. I eventually found the love of my life with my wife Michelle, but that doesn't mean there's not small remnants lurking around the heart.

Recently I was watching a series on Amazon Prime called Daisy Jones and The Six, and there she was…Olivia. I mean, it was actually the actress, Camila Morrone, but she brushed away the dust of memories covering the long-since-forgotten places in my mind.

Olivia.

Camila Morrone

Sarah Jane Perkins was a force of nature. She was a true frontier woman. She was a close relative to a Parker from the Hole in the Wall Gang. She and John Edward built the first home in Monticello, Utah, and for years the dwelling served as the Chapel and the School House. In 1987, "the family" sold the property to San Juan County. I'm not sure what "family" did that, but it certainly wasn't me, or any of my many cousins. The County knocked down the house and barn to make way for the San Juan County Jail.

For decades, Sarah Jane served in the Stake Relief Society Presidency (a women's leadership organization) while serving many terms as County Clerk and as the San Juan County delegate to the Utah Republican Party.

Bullet

Not what you think.

Riding home fast, because we were hungry, we did not notice the dog that had joined our procession. He was determined to stick with us, and at some point we became aware that we had another partner. We were flying, but he kept up with us for over a mile.

When we rolled up to our apartment, opened the door, and headed inside with our bikes, this dog darted inside our apartment, turned, and sat in the middle of our front room waggingly looking up at us as if to say, "Hey, is this where we all live?" Gotta love such confidence.

The dog had no collar, so there was no way to tell where he really belonged; he was a super cute little guy. He was clean and did not look like he lived on the street, so we knew he belonged to someone. We took his picture and made flyers that we put up around the area where he joined us, but after a month, no one claimed him. Not knowing his name, we named him Bullet...he was that fast.

He became our mission apartment pet. We fed him and took him on walks in the mornings and in the evenings so he could relieve himself. He was house-trained, but we were gone a lot during the day. We made it a point to try to come home at lunch, so Bullet could go potty.

After a while, we just let him go out with us. He would run along the sidewalk wherever we were going, then he'd wait by our bikes, guarding them, while we went inside a house or apartment to teach.

Bicycle theft was the plague for missionaries, so we welcomed Bullet's contribution. Make yourself indispensable...Bullet was a born leader.

He bed-hopped at night between my and Branham's bed, so that was nice. Long before the era of emotional support animals, it was cool to have a pet in the apartment.

At some point, we determined that as fun as it was to have Bullet, it was not practical over the long haul. He had become famous in the Zone, and Elders would come over on P-day (preparation day...Monday) to say hi, play with, and hang with Bullet. He was a good dude. The only argument Branham and I ever had was about who would get the dog in the divorce...meaning, when we eventually would be split up as missionary companions. So, it was tough to consider sending him away.

There was a family in the Ward who had four little kids…ages 3-10. We talked to the parents and told them we had this dog living with us, which they thought was hilarious. We asked if they would maybe like to take him. They were reluctant, but we talked them into meeting him knowing that if they did, it was a lock. Bullet had charisma. Sure enough, they came over, and Bullet left with them.

We got to visit him from time to time while I was in North Hollywood, and he was happy; though I'm sure Bullet would be happy regardless of his circumstances. That was just how he rolled.

Bullet!

Sarah Jane and John Edward had five children. The youngest, Linsey Claire Rogerson, went by the name "Digger," because he was the head groundskeeper on the BYU campus forever. I was 13 when he died. There are so many memories of him. Mostly, I remember he was tall...at least 6'7" or more, but to me he looked 10-feet tall. Being 6'6", I like to think I inherited height from him. He had great stories that would captivate me and my cousins for hours. One of my two prized possessions is a turquoise bolo he always wore. The other is an 1893 pump-action shotgun...the first pump action shotgun ever made. It was purchased brand new by my great-great-grandfather Benjamin Shipley Dale.

Gordon Jump, Cow-eye Soup...

...and David Lee Roth. Branham and I were at a 7-11 on Vineland getting ice cream when we saw a red Corvette come screaming into the parking lot. A guy got out wearing nothing but jogging shorts and running shoes. He left his car door open with music blaring and went straight to a pay phone. As he was talking, he noticed us staring at him, and the look of horror on his face was palpable. We kept our distance and just watched him. He finished his call, jumped back in his car, and before he sped away, he looked over and said, "Thank you;" which clearly meant, "Thanks for not hassling me."

We got a call from the sister missionaries in the southern half of North Hollywood that they needed us to help with a baptism. Turns out, they had been teaching the personal secretary to Gordon Jump. For those of you too young to remember, Gordon Jump played the Station Manager in the 70s sitcom

WKRP in Cincinnati. My generation LOVED that show. I mean, who didn't want to be as cool as Dr. Johnny Fever, or wish that Jennifer Marlowe was their secretary? Well, Gordon Jump was a well-known member of The Church of Jesus Christ of Latter-day Saints.

Brother Jump was also famous for being Peter (of Peter, James, and John) in the original, or close to the original, Temple endowment film. So, when we showed up at the baptism of his personal secretary, we were meeting a hero/celebrity on two fronts. He was super cool and down to earth.

My recollection of that night is when he confirmed his personal secretary, I remember thinking, "Wow, she's getting the Gift of the Holy Ghost from Peter himself!"

Soon thereafter we had a dinner appointment with a family. They put on the table a type of soup I had never seen before. It was purple and it had a big lump in the middle. I leaned over to my companion and whispered, "What is that?" He shrugged. No clue.

The father, noticing our whispering, smiled and said, "Es ojo de vaca," or "It's cow-eye soup."

Ok, now, never having eaten cow-eye soup, I had no idea what to do. I did notice that my companion's soup and mine were the only two with the lumps...everyone else at the table just had purple broth. Which made sense, as it would get pretty grueling for the cows to provide eyes for all eight of us. Turns out the cow-eyes are a delicacy, and they're expensive, for obvious reasons.

WKRP in Cincinnati

Do I cut into it? If I do, and the eye-innards leak into the soup, I have just magnified my problem. Do I just plop it into my mouth whole? If I do, and it pops like a cherry tomato, I might have an epileptic seizure and spit it across the room. If it oozes out like an overly ripe tomato, then that's just gross.

I took a deep breath, like a cliff diver right before jumping, and decided to bite into it whole. The insides had the texture of caviar, and it did not taste that bad. I actually liked it, and it was nice knowing I would not be offered more. The soup was black bean, but for some reason had a purple tint. The family was intrigued by our fascination and trepidation. They may have even laughed openly at us while we muddled through eating a simple soup.

Digger married Inez Hurst in 1916. They had 8 children.

Inez, or "Granner" as she was known, was born in Colónia Dublán, Mexico, to George Hurst and Mary Terry. George Hurst was one of twenty children born to Philip Hurst and his two wives, Lucinda Guymon and Elizabeth Wilcox. Philip fled to Mexico in the 1890s to avoid imprisonment for polygamy. Since our Hurst line comes from Elizabeth, we are descendants of a "second wife."

Granner, along with her parents and siblings, lived in the state of Chihuahua until the eve of the Mexican Revolution. Inez's father, George, was a blacksmith to Benito Juarez, who warned the family of imminent danger. Grandma and Grandpa Hurst cut off all the girls' hair, dressed them up like their brothers, and crossed back over into the United States on horseback, settling in San Juan County, Utah.

Granner was 17. Six years later, she married Digger.

DeFiguerido

I got the call on a Monday night about six months into my time in the mission field. I was with Branham in North Hollywood. We had had a lot of success, but things were starting to plateau, so the phone call came just at the right time. Branham was being transferred to South Pasadena, and I was getting a new missionary. I was pumped. Branham got all packed up, and the Zone Leaders came and picked us up. They dropped Branham off at his new pad on the way to taking me to the Mission President's home in Arcadia.

It was good to be back in the president's home. The last time I was there, I was a "greenie;" or new missionary. Now, I had some wear on my shoes and some smog damage to my name tag. When I walked in, Sister Meier said that all the new trainers went for a walk around the neighborhood to look at the peacocks, and she asked if I wanted to run and catch up with them. When I declined, she invited me to sit in the front room while President Meier finished a phone call.

A few minutes later, President Meier emerged. He really did look like a clean-shaven Santa Claus. He was easily the nicest man I had known in my life up to that point. When he saw me, his face lit up…confirming that I was his absolute favorite missionary. "Hey, Elder Dale, come on in!" He motioned welcomingly into his office.

We conversed briefly about how I was doing, our area in North Hollywood, and how my family was doing. Suddenly, he said, "Elder, I feel impressed to let you choose your own greenie."
"Um, ok," I stammered a bit.
"Great," he lit up again with a big smile. "Ok, as you know, we usually assign new missionaries to their trainers after a considerable amount of prayer. I recommend you start a silent prayer yourself, so that you're sure you get the new missionary you're meant to train."

Gulp…"Ok." Silent prayer quickly initiated.

About that time, I could hear the front door open and a loud herd of missionary noises.

President Meier smiled, winked, and said, "I'm guessing they're back." He was already to the door of his office before finishing the sentence.

When I rounded the corner behind him, it was like a long-lost family reunion; hearty hellos, hugs, and high-fives. There's nothing like a mission gathering, especially when you've been in the trenches with a lot of those guys.

President Meier settled us all down eventually. He said that when the new missionaries arrived, we'd all be assigned, but that would happen after an unusual first-step. "We're going to let Elder Dale choose his new missionary. This is unusual, so we will see how the afternoon goes." I understood the translation of his comment to be he would have to pick up the pieces after Dale picks the wrong guy.

We sat quietly and talked for a few more minutes until all the new missionaries came in. I had a flashback to six months prior when I walked in and first saw a room full of experienced, grizzled, veteran missionaries. Now I know that we all were just sitting there, like those before us with barely a clue about what the heck we were doing. These new ones walked in, all wide-eyed, and quickly found a seat while looking us veterans over. Probably noticing how trashed our shoes were.

President Meier again explained that I was going to choose my new missionary to train. I stood, looked around the room, and said, "I want to meet each of you and shake your hands. Please tell me your name and where you're from." I made my way around the room shaking each Elder's hand. I shook hands with all the new sisters too, though clearly picking one of them was out of the question.

About half way around, there was a tall, square-jawed, athletic-looking Elder. He looked like a good dude, so I was thinking that he was an obvious choice. I got to the end, ready to point his way, when I said "Elder DeFiguerido." He was not the stud I thought I'd pick, but a frumpy, egg-shaped, nearly bald, older looking Elder from Chicago. First, I usually don't get along with people from Chicago; it's chemical, not personal. Secondly, I'm not into nerds, and he had "IT guy" written all over his over-40 gut. So, saying his name was a bit of a shock to everyone…the other Elders in the room…President Meier…Elder DeFiguerido…me…

Without much blinking, President Meier waved me and DeFiguerido into his office. "Ok, let me meet with you two a minute, then we'll get the rest of you assigned." He welcomed us into his office, and I sat in the same chair across from his desk...now with this new Elder, DeFiguerido, sitting next to me.

President Meier asked DeFiguerido what happened when he walked off the plane today. "Well," said my new greenie, "one of your assistants walked up to me on the tarmac, and said I needed to swap this out..." He went on to describe how the A.P.s removed the English name tag from his pocket, and replaced it with a Spanish name tag.

President Meier went on to explain that DeFiguerido had just completed his MTC training in Provo after three weeks to come to Arcadia as an English Elder...an Anglo! "Elder Dale," the President said, "when we prayerfully considered trainers for this transfer, your name kept coming up. But concerned for your small amount of time in the Mission, we did not include you. When the list was done and the meeting over, I was unsettled, but it was too late to call back my assistants to the office. When I opened my door, the assistants were standing outside. 'Let's include Elder Dale in this transfer.' I said we did not have enough Spanish coming in, but we had an unassigned English Elder. If we switched his language to Spanish on arrival, it would work out. So that's what we did."

He held up a type-written roster on his desk to show me right at the top where they had typed DeFiguerido's name, that he would be Spanish, and then my name right there next to it as his trainer. Later I realized that the lesson was for DeFiguerido...not me...so that the new Elder would know the decision to go Spanish was inspired.

 MTC

Granner and Digger moved to Provo, Utah.

When my Gram, Phyllis Rogerson, was born in 1922, they had settled into a beautiful house at 55West, 4th South that is no longer there. I have a few memories of that house. Digger would call me over as he laid almost flat in his recliner and say, "Smell my feet, they smell like roses."

I never knew Granner, as she died a year before I was born.

The Ride

Still at the home of the Mission President, we loaded up my greenie's stuff in the mission van. Traditionally, incoming Elders bought the bikes of the outgoing Elders, but DeFiguerido had brought his own bike. I don't know why…I really don't…but it rubbed me the wrong way. Later, in the Army, Drill Sergeants would get mad if a troop showed up with a shaved head. Why would a recruit do that? The haircut is the job of the Army. "Do you think you are smarter than the process?"

DeFiguerido told me that the bike belonged to the older brother of the Elder who had recently baptized him. Turns out DeFiguerido had only been a member of the Church for one year. If that wasn't unique enough, he was also older; and not just by a year or two. The man was 26 and prematurely balding, which made him look 40. I know there's a max age to serve a Mission, and he had to be close to it, but I had already imagined in my mind his application for an entitled exception…Chicago.

Just as I was working myself up into a mental lather over him, he launched into how he had a girlfriend back home, and the day he returned, they would be married. He would not shut up about her on the ride from Arcadia to North Hollywood. That and his stupid bike. By the time we disembarked at the Vineland pad, I was ready to take him back and ask for a do-over. To be clear, there was nothing overtly untoward about him. The poor guy was overjoyed to be out and serving. It was me.

I didn't put any thought into it at the time as to why I had such a negative chemical reaction to him, but in retrospect I suppose that I missed Branham. We were close and had much in common. We both saw the world through a hillbilly lens. We laughed at the same things.

DeFiguerido was from Chicago. I'll just leave it at that.

When we entered the apartment, the English Elders were there to greet us. They whooped and hollered and cheered and welcomed him to which I contributed a growling, "Drop your stuff in that room and let's go." The English Elders quietly retreated into their room. It was almost 8:00pm, and missionaries had to be in by 9:30, so my order to leave was strange. The English Elders wanted no part of whatever I was cooking up.

My plan, conceived in the van ride, was to teach DeFiguerido why that bike was a dumb idea. You see, it was an old bike…I'm guessing built in the late 60s, early 70s. A Schwinn, yeah, but it must have weighed 80 pounds, had fenders and a handle bar basket, no gears, and a huge seat. I tried to tell him that the bike would kill him, but he would not listen…so I'd make him listen.

I told him we had a teaching appointment and to follow me. He was so excited, poor guy. We took off up Vineland, headed west on Roscoe to Coldwater Canyon then turned south…I had decided to ride him around the boundary of our area.

He could not catch up, so I would ride ahead to an imaginary point of "we're still together, even though we're not." It is also a non-negotiable safety rule to stay together as mission companions at all times. Stopping and waiting, he would finally ride up on that horrible contraption out of breath. The minute he'd catch up, I'd say, "Ok, let's go, can't be late."

After going south on Coldwater a bit, I turned into a neighborhood, picked out a house that was completely dark, pulled up and took out my planner as if checking the imaginary appointment time and address. As DeFiguerido pulled up I said, "Darn, looks like they're not home," before taking off again. Back out on Coldwater, we rode…fast, all the way down to Victory before heading east again over to Vineland.

The trip took us past the 90 minutes, and we rolled into the apartment around 9:45. DeFiguerido was the walking dead. He was beat. Not particularly athletic and being shaped like a pear…probably from sitting at a desk in the job at IBM he kept trying to tell me about…the man was not ready to fight the streets of North Hollywood on a bike. He may not have ever known of his lack of preparedness, had it not been for the maniac trainer (me) assigned to him. Nonetheless, he kept that ridiculous bike.

His mattress and box springs were on the floor in our room with his packed suitcase still on top. I told him to go in and unpack while I made us something to eat. About 10 minutes later, I walked in with a plate of chicken, rice, and beans to find him slumped over sideways sound asleep. He apparently sat down on the mattress with his back against the wall, but had fallen asleep sitting up before gravity got him, and pulled him over by the top of his big head.

I almost felt sorry for him, but I wasn't done yet being a jerk.

> Completely on brand as a true Harrison-Perkins-Hurst woman, my Gram was a force of nature.
>
> She married William Conant in September, 1941, just before her 19th birthday. She and Bill had 3 children. The middle child was my mother Mary Inez (a great name with true pioneer-frontier meaning).
>
> Bill flew weather missions over Normandy prior to the invasion on June 6, 1944. After the war, he continued to fly missions over the North Pole into the Soviet Union. They divorced when my Mom was 13.
>
> I never met or knew Bill.

The Jerk

Just before DeFiguerido arrived, Branham and I had baptized a single female named Evelyne del Rosario Gutierrez (Evie) who lived over on "our" street - Strathern. She was super cute and fun, and she was really excited about being a member of the Church. I made arrangements with her to play a practical joke on DeFiguerido, but now it took on a different tone. I was breaking him down and breaking him in…with no regrets.

After tracting all day, which I had not done since Widdup in Burbank, we headed over to Evie's house. It did occur to me, as I made DeFiguerido knock on doors, that maybe Widdup had done the same to me in order to break me down and break me in, but I didn't care. This new guy was going to do The Work.

What made it a challenge, is DeFiguerido did not speak any Spanish. So, I wrote out a short testimony in Spanish on a card, and told him to learn it. If we were teaching someone, I would point to him during the discussion, and he would read the card with his testimony…and cry. Every time. Yes, it was heartfelt and endearing…and moved everyone we taught to tears…but as a human, if I decided that I did not like someone, then everything was irritating. The crying made me nuts. *Dude, you're a grown man…like twice my age. Get it together.*

We pulled up to Evie's house, locked up our bikes and knocked on her door. She answered…denim mini skirt, white tank top and pony-tailed with a big smile and greeted me with a big hug. She gave DeFiguerido a big hug also, rubbed the top of his balding head and said, "Ay tan guapo, mi amor." So handsome, my love.

We went inside, and she offered us both a Miller Lite in bottles that she had drained and filled with ginger ale. She gave me a kiss on the cheek as she handed me a bottle, and ran her hand on DeFiguerido's chest and shoulder as she sat his "beer" down in front of him.

I took a big swig of mine and thanked her for it. It had been a long, hard, hot day, and I loved a good "beer" after so much preaching. I tried not to look at DeFiguerido the whole time because I might lose it, but I could feel the panic oozing out of him. You see, good Mormons don't drink alcohol.

After some flirtatious small-talk, I said I needed to go to the restroom. I got up and left the kitchen, walked around a corner, and went down the hall. I did not go into the restroom, but shut the door as if I had, then came back to listen in. You see, two missionaries are never supposed to be in different rooms…ever…ESPECIALLY in the home of a young Latin girl.

From around the corner, I could easily hear Evie trying to talk to DeFiguerido, but he couldn't understand her. Truth be told, her English was excellent, but he did not know that. I could see her but not him, and she was really pouring on the charm. At one point she extended her bare foot under the table and tried to put it in his lap. He almost jumped out of his skin. At this, she faked anger and offense, and started to yell at him.

I quickly tip-toed back into the restroom, flushed the toilet, ran some quick sink water (the yelling was really loud now), and rushed back into the kitchen to see Evie slapping DeFiguerido all about his head and shoulders. He had both his arms over his head to ward off the slaps, and he looked like he wanted to die.

I came in and said, "What the heck happened?" She wheeled on me and I told her to step back in Spanish. DeFiguerido was now trying to explain that she made a pass at him, to which I said, "that's impossible." By the way, I had not told DeFiguerido that Evie was a brand-new member of the Church, but that she was taking the lessons and thinking about joining. So, he thought he had really messed this up, and now she would hate the Church.

She continued to carry on, in a very convincing way, telling us we had to leave. As she was kicking us out, I reach to grab my "beer" and finish it off. For effect, I grabbed DeFiguerido's too and chugged it. He was aghast as she continued to chew his butt out in a language he couldn't understand.

Now on the front porch, she's yelling and throwing shoes at us. DeFiguerido hit the door and ran to the sidewalk where his bike was chained up. I walked a few steps and turned back. Evie then switched to English and said, "Wow, Elder Dale, thank you, that was fun." I smiled back and said, "Yeah Evie, new missionary pranks have to be memorable, and this certainly was. You're too funny. Thanks for the ginger ale, but next time I'll drink it from the ginger ale can, ok?" She laughed at that.

Turning around, I saw DeFiguerido standing by his bike, jaw dropped as he processed what just happened. Instead of laughing and admitting he'd been had, he jumped on his bike and tried to speed away; which he could have, if his bike wasn't such a piece of garbage.

I let him ride in front of me for a while until he figured out he had no idea where he was or where he was going. He simply stopped his bike and started to cry. Again. If you think this is the part where I ride up and have some soothing words of wisdom that will lift his spirits and inspire him, think again.

I rode by him slowly and said, "You should really pay attention to the routes when we ride, so you know how to get back to our pad." I rode a while before looking back to see if he was still with me. I figured either he was going to come along or not, but he had to choose. He was there. I'm sure he was riding behind me thinking of ways to kill me in my sleep...with a calculator...or smother me with a pocket protector.

Here's THE IRONY of my Mission: DeFiguerido and I baptized...a lot. In fact, I had more baptisms with him than any one of my other companions.

How I spent my 20th birthday.

> Gram moved all around the world with Bill and her children during World War II. After they divorced, she settled in Northern Arizona as a single Mom in 1950s America. Not easy, but Gram was formidable. She got to work getting her degree, while working in the County Assessor's office. Grandma Perkins would have been proud. After a brief marriage to Myrlan Brown, his death left her single again.
>
> Using the tax rolls, she researched the ten wealthiest bachelors in Apache County.
>
> That's how she met, and soon married, Bert Colter.

November '86

I had been serving in the North Hollywood 4th Ward now for three months, and Branham and I had been very successful baptizing maybe a dozen people by that time. We had a huge teaching pool, so the prospects were promising. But then, the bottom dropped out. By the third week of November, DeFiguerido and I had no one. All our good teaching prospects had gone away...dried up. No one.

Sure, Branham and I came into the area with nothing and built something out of it, but this step back to square one was scary; it had me in a panic. Some of you might say that it was my fault for being such a jerk to DeFiguerido. Maybe... but at that time I was not very self-aware. I did not know what to do, so I took it to the Lord.

Again, after lights out, I slipped out of bed onto my knees and began to appeal to my Heavenly Father in the hopes of getting some answers as to what was happening. We could not get anyone to open the door to us. As it is said in the military, the area was "comms out." The Mission had added another pair of missionaries to the Ward, and they were doing great. It was us, and I did not know why.

For the second time on my Mission, I waited for my companion to fall asleep before praying privately. I don't know why I was shy about my mission companions seeing me pray individually. Yet, as I prayed, these words came clearly into my mind as though pressed into my head with an ice pick: "Where is your Book of Mormon?" That was a strange thing to have come to me, so I kept praying for understanding. Again, "Where is your Book of Mormon?"

I got up and started looking for it, but sure enough, I was unable to find my copy. Now curious, I started looking everywhere. Finally, I looked under my bed. Yes, I had a bed frame and DeFiguerido did not. When Branham moved out, one of the English Elders wanted his frame, and I let him take it. Under my frame, way in the back against the wall, was my personal copy of The Book of Mormon. I struggled to retrieve it, went into the bathroom, and started to read. Soon my eyes, mind, and heart were drawn to Alma 46:8:

> Thus we see how quick the children of men do forget the Lord their God, yea, how quick to do iniquity, and to be led away by the evil one.

Yes, that was me. I had forgotten who's Work it was. Now I had a testimony that God was leading our Work, and Jesus Christ was the message. I went back into the bedroom to resume my prayer and ask for forgiveness; however, before I could get a word out, the same voice came into my mind saying, "If you stay close to The Book of Mormon, I will open up the heavens and pour out blessings upon you."

I was so excited to have an answer that I woke up DeFiguerido, "Elder, I know what's wrong. I know why we don't have anyone to teach. It's The Book of Mormon...we need to read it more!"

For those unfamiliar, that's a ridiculous thing to say. It's like saying, "I know why we can't get this building painted, we need paint!"

Elder DeFiguerido, though new, understood this to be ridiculous also, and said, "Good one, yeah right, The Book of Mormon. Why didn't I think of that?" He rolled back toward the wall and continued to snore. Starting the next day, I began each morning study session by reading 20-30 minutes in The Book of Mormon. That was a big change, considering I was neck deep in doctrinal materials outside of the scriptures. In the Doctrinal New Testament Commentary by Bruce R. McConkie, I was learning so much about the Gospel; what the Lord was trying to tell me was to place an emphasis and importance on The Book of Mormon. So, I did.

In short order, we had a full teaching pool again. We were busy. There were six lessons a person needed from the missionaries before being baptized, and each lesson was about an hour long. By the first week of December, we were teaching ten lessons per day, easily. We were teaching from sun up to sun down, eating fast food on the way to appointments. We had no time for anything. It got so crazy that we were only teaching the first four discussions before turning lessons 5 and 6 over to the local Ward part-time missionaries whose job, or "calling," was to assist the full-time missionaries. The last week of December, we only taught first and second discussions before moving on to the next person on our list. It was nuts.

In the month of December, we set mission records in teaching and came close to the baptismal record of 21. The third week of December we taught 45 full discussions. We baptized 19 people that month, including 5 on Christmas Day.

Message received. All in all, DeFiguerido and I would have 27 baptisms together in December 1986 and January 1987. We never did really get along, but we had incredible success. At the end of January, we both left North Hollywood, but our paths would cross again.

For all us cousins, Bert Colter was our grandpa. He was a real cowboy.

The Colters were original Arizonians, and at one time they just about owned all the land, along with their rivals, the Udall Family. Bert was a wealthy rancher, a state Senator, and a fascinating man. He was 35 years older than Gram.

My favorite story is when he fell off his horse, sliced off his ear on a rock, put the ear in a handkerchief, and rode through the night to Shiprock, New Mexico, where there was a doctor who could sew it back on.

We would listen to his stories for hours.

Thanksgiving

Dinner appointments were the life blood of every missionary. Eating Ramen and Hungry Man stew with hot dogs every day was no way to live, so the local members feeding the missionaries is imperative. Let me tell you, serving among the Latino people meant eating great. The people we served did not have much in terms of worldly possessions, but they would give us their last bit of food if they had it. Every home we visited had a pot of beans on and a big pot of rice going all the time. Homemade tortillas were the norm, and we would eat them with beef, chicken or lamb. Experienced missionaries also became quickly adept at sensing menudo from the sidewalk outside, and that smell would send us running the other way.

I was determined to master getting dinner appointments.

My main tactic in obtaining dinner appointments (referred to as a D.A.) was to use what I called "D.A. face." By this time on the Mission, I was developing a pretty good one. All the best missionaries knew about this and could expertly execute one. The face, when presented to a member of the Church, would result in them asking us over to eat at their house for dinner. Simple.

It was a way of looking hungry that would hopefully elicit an invitation. My D.A. face had begun to bear fruit. In conversation with a member, I could summon the face and invariably they would offer, "So do you all have somewhere to eat today?" If we did, they would immediately offer another day that week. If we didn't, bam, we had a home cooked meal lined up that night.

Feeding the missionaries is as important as anything else you can do for them. Also, missionaries are hungry, not picky, so just make a lot of it whatever it is. If you do not have a lot to give, just make a pot full of cheap spaghetti…seriously, it doesn't matter. Missionaries want to eat.

By the time I got to the end of my Mission, I wielded the D.A. face to get, not only dinner appointments, but lunch, and the Holy Grail - the breakfast appointment. I'll be more Jordan than LeBron here, leaving it up to the pundits to determine whether my D.A. face goes on Mt. Rushmore.

These days, when sharing this story with full-time missionaries over dinner in our home, I'll try to demonstrate, but it's gone. I don't have it anymore.

I was in the early stages of mastering the D.A. face my first Thanksgiving in the mission field. The Sunday prior, the appointments started rolling in; before we knew it, DeFiguerido and I had an appointment to eat every 30 minutes from 9:30am to 9:00pm. We were packed.

When we got to the first member's home, we discovered that the Latin tradition for Thanksgiving is tamales. We had tamales from every Latin American country from Mexico to Argentina.

The best ones we ate had a pineapple square in the middle. I want to say those tamales were from Mexico. I definitely remember the worst ones were from El Salvador. They were soggy. The Peruvian tamál has an olive or a peanut in the middle; I wasn't a fan of those either, but the olive and peanut could be pushed aside for just eating the masa which was really good. The soggy ones (aguados) I could do without.

Our other challenge was that each appointment did not know we had other appointments. How could they? So, each family thought we were the only meal of the day. They wanted us to eat multiple tamales. After the first house, I knew there was no way we could do this all day. Starting with the second appointment, I only ate one. The sister in that second appointment was mildly offended until I asked her if she would bag some up for us to eat later. She lovingly loaded up a plastic grocery bag.

By the end of the night, we had a trunk full of tamales, call it two dozen bags each with a dozen tamales. It was a lot. We were driving up Tujunga toward Saticoy, when we saw people lined up outside a soup kitchen. We pulled over, got out and asked if anyone wanted fresh tamales. Dumb question. We handed them out in short order, and were back on our way...stomachs bulging.

More than 30 years later, and living in Manhattan Beach, California, a full-time missionary came into the Ward there, and I heard he came from North Hollywood. I asked him a bunch of questions about the work there, eventually bringing up the tamales we gave to the homeless outside the soup kitchen on Tujunga. "Oh yeah," he said, "the Spanish Elders still do that there."

He said it's a big deal, and the members will cook extra for the missionaries to take with them to the homeless in that area.

Pretty cool.

North Hollywood Soup Kitchen

Gram finally became a 3rd grade teacher and eventually the principal of Round Valley Elementary School. By the time she retired in the late 1980s, she was a local legend. Everyone had been her student…and their kids…and their kids kids.

When I was having trouble with an Elder Ashcroft on my Mission, who was from Round Valley, I told Gram over the phone one Christmas from Echo Park.

"He used to pee his pants and cry all the time."

Though I never repeated it, knowing that made it easier to deal with him.

Frequent Stops

THE BEST BURRITO in the Arcadia Mission is on the corner of Lankershim and Sherman Way. *El Michoacano* is a spot about as big as your Mom's kitchen. It has one window, and during the time I was there, no places to sit. I think there are benches there now. There're enough parking spots for maybe five cars now. Back then, it was for locals. You walked up and bought a $2 burrito the size of Hulk Hogan's forearm. They tasted amazing.

There used to be nothing around it but industrial office buildings. Now, there's a sit-down restaurant across the street called *Carnitas Michoacán*. Don't be fooled by this imposter of a place. The real spot is across the street…the low-down-dive looking place. *El Michoacano* is the genuine article.

When we would roll up, the large woman inside would greet us warmly in Spanish, "Hi Elders, the usual?"

"Yes, ma'am," we would say through drooling lips from the wonderful smell as we placed a *fiver* on the counter. The finished product filled with carne asada, rice, beans, salsa, guac, and wrapped in a homemade tortilla would slide through the window wrapped in tin foil. An horchata to go, and we would be on our way.

"Bye Elders, be careful out there."

"Yes ma'am."

I returned to *El Michoacano* in 1996 with my wife Michelle, nearly ten years removed from my time in North Hollywood. Dressed in a polo and khakis, I rolled up for my now $5 burrito. I leaned down into the window to see the same lady making the food. Before I could state my order, she said, "Hi Elder, the usual?" I was speechless. Now that's a connection to your customers.

I beamed and said, "Yes ma'am!" It was fun to introduce my wife to her and express how happy I was to be back at her place eating a burrito that, not only tasted amazing, but brought back so many wonderful memories.

The other frequent stop we discovered while in North Hollywood was the L.A. County Courthouse in downtown Los Angeles. Occasionally, the families we taught, and who expressed a desire to be baptized, were couples who were not married. They couldn't be baptized if they were living together without being married.

California has a common law marriage stipulation on the books, but the Church only recognized civil marriages at the time. People who were in the United States without documents would not get married legally due to a fear of going to the courthouse to get the license. Many of them had been living together far longer than the minimum for common law, but we had to help them with the official marriage process. So, when confronted with this challenge, we did what any good missionaries would do: we loaded them up in our car and took them to the courthouse to get their marriage license. We had to balance getting the job done with breaking mission rules.

First, the courthouse was outside our Mission…not just our assigned area, but the whole Arcadia Mission! Downtown L.A. was in the Los Angeles Mission. Once we crossed Sunset, we were breaking the rules. Also, putting civilians in the mission car was expressly forbidden. Not only were these people civilians, they were not even members of the Church, yet!

I'm sure other Elders did the same, but no one ever talked about it. We just did it. The decision for me was not difficult. We had people who wanted to join themselves to the body of the Saints. There was no way I was letting a mission boundary rule stop me. As life would go on, I would discover that I am definitely an "ends guy," as in, *the end justifies the means*. If the proposed end is something good for people or communities, I'll always - without hesitation - do whatever it takes to achieve that good result.

Over the course of more than a year, I'm betting we transported more than a dozen couples to the courthouse. They were incredibly nervous…standing in line…in a government courthouse without legal documents. All of them had falsified identification: driver's licenses and Social Security cards.

Again, we did not bat an eye. When asked, we told the attendant at the window we were there to translate…which we were, but our overall role was far more than that. We would do whatever it took to help these people become members of the church.

Ok, we were down for whatever.

As the Matriarch, Gram set the moral standard in the family. She taught us all what it meant to be members of the Church. We knew full well that the blood of Mormon Pioneers, through several lineage lines, flowed through our veins. She instilled an expectation, a responsibility if you will, that we all had by birthright, to live our lives by Gospel Standards. She vetted every date. I cannot tell you how many times I heard, "you can't date her, that family never amounted to anything." My cousins grew up near her, so they had it much worse than me.

She once tried to talk me out of a date with Miss Teen Utah. Frustrated by it, I responded, "I don't want to marry her, I just want to make out with her. A lot."

I carry the guilt of that disrespectful remark to this day.

Confessions of a District Leader

After riding bikes around for just over a month, DeFiguerido and I got a mission car. The reason for that change was I had been assigned, or "called," as we say, to be a District Leader. Our well-used Toyota Corolla got us around just fine. I did not know it at the time, but I would have a car for the rest of my time in the mission field. I would only be on a bike for about ten weeks of my two years. Pretty sad compared to most missionaries who walk or bike the entire time.

I quickly learned the responsibilities of a District Leader:

1. Report weekly to the Zone Leaders the progress/success of each pair (normally 4-5) of missionaries in the District.

2. Conduct monthly training sessions with the District based on the training received from the Zone Leaders, who had been trained by the Assistants to the President (A.P.s).

3. Conduct baptismal interviews for those being baptized within the District.

4. Resolve concerns or conflicts between companionships should they arise.

It was the last one that I was unprepared to handle. Looking back with 50-year-old eyes, how in the world was a 20-year-old kid supposed to give advice to anyone? It was on the job training for sure.

Sitting in the apartment, grabbing a quick bite, the phone rang. It was a sister missionary up in La Cañada named Sister Downs. She was crying and panicking. She was hyperventilating when she told me that she was locked in the bathroom, and her companion, Sister Pearce was going to kill her.

She then screamed and hung up.

Not knowing what to do, I just said to DeFiguerido that we needed to go. It took a good 30 minutes to get to their apartment, which is pretty impressive, but we were driving aggressively. It had been raining in La Cañada, and the main street in town was a river-torrent of run-off.

We pulled up to the sister missionaries' house and ran up to the door. I looked inside and saw Sister Pearce with a knife. I kicked open the door, and that startled her. She dropped the knife and started to cry…not a sad cry, but a mad cry.

We got both sisters in the living room and asked what happened. They both sobbed through a story that started when they passed by the apartment to get a pamphlet they needed. It was raining really hard, and there was a heated discussion about who was going to go in and get the pamphlet. It was decided that Sister Pearce, who we saw with the knife, would go in. La Cañada is very hilly, so when she put her foot out of the car, the torrent of rain water took her shoe down the street. She took off running after it, and after some effort, returned back to the car to find Sister Downs still sitting behind the wheel having not retrieved the pamphlet from their apartment. That really set Sister Pearce off, and a fight ensued that started outside the car after Sister Pearce grabbed Downs by the back of the head and tried to shove her into the water cascading down the street. This scuffle spilled into the house. Sister Pearce swore up and down that the knife was to pick the lock, pry open the door of the restroom, but not to stab her companion.

So, what to do? On a whim I said they needed to pray for each other so I directed them to kneel and take turns praying, asking for a blessing on, and expressing love for their companion by name. They refused, so I turned to DeFiguerido and said, "Wow, President Meier didn't tell us what to do if they refused." I hadn't called President Meier, but DeFiguerido played along shrugging his shoulders.

I told DeFiguerido to call President Meier and ask what we should do.

As he got up to go use their phone, the sisters quickly changed their tune, buying my bluff. They took turns praying for each other. Not sincerely, but they did it. We sat a bit longer while they calmed down. They slowly broke down even more and apologized to each other. We got a sense that they were fine.

Thankfully, they were in fact fine.

Many times, I've asked myself why I didn't call 911, or why I didn't call the Zone Leaders, the A.P.s or the President? Why didn't I call their Bishop? I don't know, and I don't have a good answer. In the end it worked out, and I know that if I would have called any of those people, the two sisters would probably have been sent home. It was good they weren't; thus, allowing them to finish out their missions. I just reacted, not thinking it through, and it worked out.

Sisters Downs and Pearce eventually became great friends.

To drive home the concept and the importance of "enduring to the end," Gram would tell a story about her grandfather, John Edward Rogerson. Enduring to the end is a principle of devotion requiring that a disciple of Jesus Christ live righteously to the final day of their life. It was a big Gram doctrine.

You see, Grandpa Rogerson never swore, ever…but on the day he died, his final words were laced with profanity to the shock, dismay, and horror of his vast family, who were all gathered at his deathbed. As little kids, us cousins would just nod dutifully, never wanting to fall from grace like our great-great-grandfather. Surely, we could redeem him through our faithfulness.

As adults, we asked Gram what he actually said. With much nervousness and sadness, having to relive the horror, she said, "He sat up in his bed and said, 'It's a damn shame when a man can't go out and get a load of wood for his family.' Then he laid back down and died."

Even my Utah cousins were all, "That's it!?!" For my part, I sat there thinking, "Man, if they only knew the prolific use of language by the Dale side of my family."

A Vision

P-day or preparation day is a wonderful time in the life of a missionary. Every Monday, missionaries around the world do their laundry, clean their apartment, write letters (now call) home, go grocery shopping (and some thrifting), and get haircuts. But the biggest event on P-day is the universal pastime of missionaries - basketball.

Basketball is the official game of all Mormons. We love it, can't get enough of it. And it is very…very competitive. What's the only fight that starts with a prayer? A Mormon pick-up game of basketball. For a time in the late 70s early 80s, the most prominent part of an LDS chapel building complex was the gym. Someone in Salt Lake must have eventually said out loud that it was probably sending the wrong message to the world.

We are a strong Christian faith that gets accused of being a cult that worships Joseph Smith, rejects the Bible for the Book of Mormon, and still practices polygamy. All of those things are false. We worship God and believe that the head of our Church is Jesus Christ. We believe the Bible to be scripture and the Book of Mormon to be a companion book of scripture, also testifying of Jesus Christ. We do not worship Joseph Smith. So, the last thing we need is people believing we love basketball more than God. I mean the Baptists and football, yeah, but not us with basketball. So, the huge gyms attached to chapels have been better camouflaged in chapel constructions over the years.

The P-day basketball games in North Hollywood were epic. So much so, that bodies started flying around too much, and guys were getting hurt. At some point during my two years, full-court was outlawed, because of all the busted knees and ankles. Pretty sure we all kept doing it, but we knew if anyone got hurt, we were all in a lot of trouble.

One P-day, after a grueling session of round ball, I was walking through the church building looking for DeFiguerido. He did not play, of course, so I had no idea where he was for the two hours I was putting in work on the court. Half-way down the hall and outside the Relief Society Room, I heard crying…like serious, sobbing, crying. I opened the door to see DeFiguerido lying completely face down on the floor.

I went right over to him, thinking he was hurt, injured, or something. He noticed I was there, rolled over and sat up. "What are you doing? Are you ok?" I really did not know what to ask. He continued to cry but told me that no matter how hard he prayed, he could not get the Savior to appear to him. He felt that he needed the Savior to visit him, or he did not know if he could go on. On some level, I knew what he was going through from the experience with my own testimony in Burbank.

I had no idea what to do or what to say. This was beyond my maturity level and skill set by a country mile. I just remember feeling compassion for him for the first time. He was so sad and so sincere. I did manage to tell him that it was unlikely to happen, so somehow he had to find a way to carry on. I said that if the Savior had a reason to visit him, He would; if not, no amount of praying would force Him to appear. I told him I was sorry that he felt he needed that, and I hoped he could make it through.

He did.

Not that he needed it or sought for it, but his sincere desire to be close to the Savior softened my heart toward him. All of us, with so many differences on the outside, basically want the same thing. To know that God lives, Jesus is His son and that after we die, we can return to them.

My Mom knew all too well that Gram would in no way shape or form approve of the skirt chasing outlaw from Kansas, who was just passing through town, so my Mom and Dad eloped.

They drove two hours from St. Johns to Flagstaff late Sunday night, May 31, 1964 to find the Stake President. Once on his doorstep, this poor Stake President refused to marry them. "Sister Conant {Gram} will kill me if I marry you like this." My Mom did not flinch, "not as bad as she will kill you if we have to go to the Justice of the Peace."

He married them *post haste*.

Holidays

There were lonely times on my Mission, for sure. Sometimes there was a feeling of "Will this ever end." There was a constant feeling of missing out as the world continued on, in spite of me not being in it. Sometimes there were disappointments that made me question why I was out there. I got homesick, and missed my friends, and sometimes felt like my life was passing me by while I was toiling away. Then there were Holidays.

Back then, missionaries were only allowed to call home on Mother's Day and Christmas. The rest of the time it was letters only. I did not write much, ironically, though I wrote my parents every week. My Mom wrote back occasionally, but surprisingly, my Dad wrote to me every week.

I say "surprisingly" because my Dad, though a member of the Church, was not very active. He joined the Church in 1964 two years before I was born, because my Mom said she wouldn't marry him unless he got baptized. A nominal Catholic, he easily made that bet. Dad was a real cowboy and half an outlaw. That should remove some doubts about me for those who know me.

At the water's edge of baptism, my Dad was ordained an Elder, and was set apart as Branch Mission Leader and a Counselor in the Branch Presidency...all incredibly unusual for a brand new member. Two years later, he graduated from Ft. Hays State with a degree in Finance, and he and my Mom loaded me up and moved to New Mexico. I was six months old.

My Dad had been through the Temple by then, as my Mom said there would be no children until they were Sealed in a Temple together. When they landed in Albuquerque where my Dad was in training for his first job with SIC Finance, he said that he would take a break from Church.

His break lasted 19 years getting slowly active again as I prepared for and served a Mission. Though he never returned to the agreed-upon full activity, my Dad never considered himself an inactive member. His letters to me in the mission field were always welcomed, and through them he would begin to say "Love Dad" at the end of the letters. It was through those letters alone that he would ever express his love out loud.

Once in a wonderful blue moon, I would get a letter from a girl. Those were great days.

Most Holidays involved eating at members' homes, and it was good to get a home cooked meal. We stayed off the streets on big drinking days...St. Patrick's and Cinco de Mayo. We watched fireworks on the 4th of July, but from the roof of our apartment. The big Holiday to stay clear of people was New Year's Eve.

Both NYE holidays on my Mission, we gathered in an Elder's apartment, drank Martinelli's at 9:00pm, and rang in the new year fellowshipping with each other on east coast time from California. We thought we were so smart circumventing the time zones to meet mission rules and still getting home by the appointed 9:30pm mission curfew.

The Mission Christmas Parties made up for some of the home sickness. They were really fun. There was music, gift exchanges, skits, and food…lots of it for the 150 or so missionaries. It was good to see old friends. My first Christmas in the Mission, it was good to see Branham. My second Christmas, I was about to go home, so there was a sense of melancholy and good-bye. Missionaries have no idea that all those close friends, those Brothers in Arms as Dire Straits so profoundly defined, would soon be faded memories.

Dire Straits - Brothers in Arms

Baptisms in the North Hollywood 4th Ward

Date	Name of Person	Baptized by:
7 Sep 86	Carmen Lola Picolomini	Sandoval
7 Sep 86	Elisa Ventura	me
7 Sep 86	Nancy Zelaya	Branham
14 Sep 86	Maria de la Serna	Branham
14 Sep 86	Isabel Pelayo Acevedo	Branham
19 Sep 86	Ramon Medoza Larios	Branham
19 Sep 86	Alma Trinidad Mendoza	Branham
19 Sep 86	David Gonzales Verduzco	me
21 Sep 86	Rolando Chacon Hernandez	me
19 Oct 86	Evelyng del Rosario Gutierrez	Branham
7 Dec 86	Cruz Maria Rivas de Martinez	me
7 Dec 86	Roberto Hernandez	me
7 Dec 86	Maria Ambrozia Lazo	me
7 Dec 86	Sylvia Maria Hernandez	DeFiguerido
13 Dec 86	Miguel Gonzalez Ramos	DeFiguerido
14 Dec 86	Juana Elizabeth Flores	Escobar
20 Dec 86	Dimas Salazar	DeFiguerido
21 Dec 86	Ismael Escobar Mazaregos	Escobar
23 Dec 86	Rosa Edith Garcia	DeFiguerido
25 Dec 86	Angelica Maria Lopez	me
25 Dec 86	Rodolfo Antonio Reyes	me
25 Dec 86	Wanda Lucretia Guembas	me
25 Dec 86	Monica Lissette Guembas	me
25 Dec 86	Christina Lisa Murrillo	DeFiguerido
27 Dec 86	Josefina de la Mora	DeFiguerido
27 Dec 86	Nancy Ivonne de la Mora	DeFiguerido
27 Dec 86	Laura de la Mora	DeFiguerido
28 Dec 86	Christina Murrillo	DeFiguerido
28 Dec 86	Mercedes Machado Beltran	DeFiguerido
11 Jan 87	Vera Edith Reyes	Boris Reyes
11 Jan 87	Tony Reyes	Reyes
25 Jan 87	Rosalinda Reyes	Reyes
25 Jan 87	Devanira Reyes	Reyes
25 Jan 87	Augustine Perez	Pozo
25 Jan 87	Maria Rosario Majano	Juan Tovar
25 Jan 87	Jorge Alberto Valencia	Juan Tovar
1 Feb 87	Carlos Ernesto Ventura	me

> Mom, being a faithful latter-day Saint, refused to marry my Dad unless he got baptized. So, he did. She then refused to have any kids with him unless he received his Temple Endowments and got Sealed to her. So, he did.
>
> I'm grateful she did that, though it obviously did not translate into his full commitment. I never doubted his Testimony or belief in the teachings of the Restored Gospel of Jesus Christ, but he just wasn't into all of it.
>
> Dad loved beer, and he had been smoking since his early teens…as in 13.

Zone 7

By December of 1986, my Zone Leader was Jim Thorderson. He was from Michigan, at least 6'8", Hollywood-handsome, and the most talented, out-going person I had known in my life up to that point. About a year ahead of me, he had been an adjacent District Leader from the southern half of North Hollywood, my Assistant Zone Leader, and my Zone Leader. All this meant that we had been around each other a lot. I was very jealous that Elder Gardner had been his companion in North Hollywood. We spent a lot of time together that December, because he was interviewing all those good people we baptized that month.

We hit it off right away, and over time started scheming how we could get Pres. Meier to put us together as companions.

Over numerous conversations, we contrived this method of encouraging local members to get involved in missionary work. We called it a "rancho," and it was basically giving people a star if they referred someone to us to be taught. It seemed revolutionary at the time but kind of dumb now. We really believed in it, and sure enough in February of 1987, I was transferred to the Del Rio Branch in Echo Park to serve as District Leader and Assistant Zone Leader with Elder Thorderson.

Elder DeFiguerido got transferred to somewhere in the San Gabriel Valley…as an English Elder! The only time in the Mission he served as a Spanish Elder was with me. He went right back to the English work. Crazy, but it was over.

My time with DeFiguerido was done, and I was glad for it. To be fair, DeFiguerido was a good guy, but I couldn't get past whatever my issues were. Whatever…it was over now, and Thorderson and I had a mindset to revolutionize missionary work. No tracting…exploring new ways to find people and lots of teaching.

After they married, Mom and Dad moved back to Hays, Kansas to a little house in the middle of town that is now a grocery store parking lot. About a year and a half later, I was born.

My Mom claims that two significant events happened the night I was born: there was a tornado that touched down near the town, and a UFO was sighted. I can find no evidence of either event. I think she was speaking euphemistically. Yes, I researched her claims.

The worst tornado in the history of Kansas occurred a year earlier in Topeka, and there was a UFO sighting earlier in 1966 on the other side of the state; nothing around my birth. It's ok, I had enough heritage to live up to, regardless.

Del Rio

The apartment in Echo Park on Lucretia was incredible. Sitting on the back wall we could see over the left field fence into Dodger stadium, and on days where there was a Monday home game, we would walk…yes walk…over, pay six bucks to sit in the upper deck, and watch a game.

Fernando Valenzuela had just come off a Cy Young year, and I would be in that area until June of 1987 to witness much of the Dodger's season on the brink. In 1988 they would win the World Series after Kirk Gibson's iconic homer. Heck, when we went to a game and sat in the upper deck, we found it was

87 Dodgers

mostly Latinos…and they knew how to party at a game. They would bring grocery bags full of food, eager to share with missionaries…especially after seeing my D.A. face.

The Del Rio Branch was a wonderful group of people. The congregation was not big enough to be a Ward, and we were determined to baptize enough people so the Church could create a Ward in that area. It was no small thing: they needed to double in size.

The leadership needed a lot of help, and we were there to assist as best we could. Thorderson and I were crazy busy; between finding people to teach, teaching, helping out in the Branch, assisting the other missionaries in the Zone, meeting with the Mission President and his Assistants…it was a lot of work.

In the late 80s, Echo Park was THE MOST dangerous area in Los Angeles. Not East L.A. (which was also in the Arcadia Mission) and not Skid Row (in the L.A. Mission). Echo Park had that distinction. It was gnarly; not the flavored coffee, skinny jeans, beanies in the summer, artsy area it is today. In 1987, Echo Park was a war zone. The Sean Penn / Robert Duvall movie *Colors* was filmed there. A chase scene in that movie shows a group of gang kids running up a hill that was right under our pad.

We were not allowed to be out after dark or one hour after sundown. That meant we had to be off the street by 6:00pm in the winter and by 8:30pm in the summer. "Off the street" meant walking around on sidewalks. If we had an appointment, we could drive to and from, but no wandering around in our car.

Gunshots, sirens, and helicopters were just white noise in the background. I did not realize how used to it I had become until I woke up in rural East Texas after my Mission. The silence was deafening. It would be years until I could be comfortable in silence, and in a lot of ways I still have not adjusted.

[106] The good news: gangs did not mess with God, who they viewed more with superstition than with devotion. The better good news there: their superstition-over-devotion culture meant it did not matter what their or your religion was. We represented some version of God; as long as we were respectful and smart, we could walk the streets of L.A. with impunity.

The curfew was to protect us from crossfire...getting caught in the middle of something, which always sparked up at night.

But...said in my best Edward James Olmos voice...I was from North Hollywood, *ese*, I ate danger for breakfast...

My Dad graduated with a Bachelor's degree in Business from Fort Hays State before my parents loaded me up in their car and heading to New Mexico. I was six months old when they moved into their first apartment in Albuquerque.

After a few short months, SIC Finance moved our little family to 905 Dewey Ln in Alamogordo, New Mexico.

The house is still there.

Tamales

I have to mention the lady down on Echo Park Avenue, near Avalon St. who sold Tamales out of her kitchen window. For a dozen tamales loaded into a Vons grocery bag, you just put your $5 cash on the window sill.

Cash business, no change. Throw up your fiver, walk away with a dozen, steaming, Mexican tamales. She put a piece of pineapple in them. So good.

I don't remember much from our first stint in Alamogordo. I have some memories of the house: my favorite stuffed animal - a pink bunny; seeing my Dad come home on crutches with a sprained ankle he suffered in a semi-pro basketball game playing point guard for the Alamogordo Buckaroos; the front yard; and the elderly couple, Harry and Donna Thomas, who lived across the street. They babysat me alot. Donna made the best oatmeal, and Harry chain smoked. It's a miracle I don't have lung cancer.

Mission Barber

Elder Graebel was an odd duck. There were times I wasn't even sure he was a missionary. In my mind, he had been on his Mission for a decade; people just forgot he was still there. He did not do any missionary work, of that I'm certain. His job? Elder Graebel was the mission mechanic.

We're known for our bikes, but in the Arcadia Mission, we had a fleet of Toyota Corollas. They had no radios in them, and we had a mileage limit per month, but they were like candy to us. I knew missionaries were on foot all over third world countries, but this was Hollywood. We rolled like movie stars in comparison.

Every Monday morning, Graebel would pull up to our apartment in a van. He and his "comp" would pile out and set up their jacks and jack stands. By 7:00am, mission cars would start rolling in. A Corolla carries five people: four passengers and a driver; however, when each car pulled up, six to eight missionaries would come falling out.

Graebel would have their hood up on the quick like a NASCAR pit crew. The first time I saw it, I was mesmerized. It was like watching Coltrane, or better yet - Lenny Bruce. If Lenny Bruce was a mechanic, he would be Graebel. The first morning I witnessed him pull the oil dipstick, lick it clean, then put it back in to get a better read. He. licked. the. dipstick. Graebel was a madman.

While that went on…changing oil and filters…and rotating tires, Thorderson cut hair. That's why all the other missionaries came along. Thorderson was the mission de facto barber. He had a pro-set of clippers, and he was really good at it. Mind you, everyone got the same basic cut, but they were done right; all looked professional when he was done.

Each haircut was $5…he could have done them for free, but President Meier asked Thorderson to charge, so he undercut the going rate at a barber shop by $1 and spent the entire morning each Monday cutting hair, or as he would say "cutting heads." Must be a Michigan thing.

He would make $100 or more a week. It was insane. He taught me how to do it, we got another set of clippers, and, bam, we expanded our operation. We made bank.

The money came in handy, because Thorderson introduced me to thrift shopping. The thrift stores in SoCal are legendary. His philosophy: hit the Goodwill or Salvation Army in or near wealthy neighborhoods; so the Salvation Army in South Pasadena and the Goodwill in Hacienda Heights were our main spots.

There were a couple of good stores in Burbank too. We tried to keep the mission rules of not leaving the Zone, but the stores beckoned.

We could hit a store, "score" a couple of suits, white shirts, ties, and shoes…literally a pile of clothes for each , and it would be no more than 40-50 bucks. We started buying non-missionary clothes too. I was a clothes horse all the way back to elementary school, and I was voted "Best Dressed" in the

Cleveland High School Senior class of 1985 along with Melinda Whitten.

So, with my pedigree, Thorderson and I were fashion soulmates. At a mission conference that Spring, we were voted the "best dressed Elders" by an overwhelming margin. We had a lot of fun with it…taking modeling photos and goofing around. I thought Branham and I were close, and we were, but Thordy and I were like brothers…literally. His 6'8" frame and my 6'6" frame created an imposing visual for members and non-members alike.

Of course, like any partnership, we did not always get along. I'll be brutally and embarrassingly honest. Thorderson was not a fan of certain smells I would produce from time to time. It's not like I ramped up my flatulence game for him, but no one had ever called me on it before. I did not think I had an issue. Until he pointed it out to me, I never knew it was a problem.

One night in our apartment, he exploded out of the blue, "DUDE, YOU HAVE A PROBLEM!" I had cut one, so I knew what he was referring to, but I was shocked at the decibel-level of his reaction. I laughed it off thinking he was joking, which made him even more mad. He just kept saying over and over, "DUDE, YOU HAVE A PROBLEM!" The more I laughed, the more emphatic he became, saying that I needed to see a doctor. He threatened to call the Mission President and demand I get help.

After 10 minutes of this argument, I finally apologized and said I would be more conscientious. He backed off a little, but I'd bet a week's worth of haircuts that he asked the Mission President to refer me to a doctor.

For my part of the partnership, it bugged me that he would come in every morning, sit down with his cereal, bow his head, and say a silent prayer over his food. It's not the praying that rubbed me wrong; it's that he did it silently, without me. I'm sitting there with my cereal patiently waiting for him to join me, then he would just go without me. Can't we pray over the food together?

So, I said something. Yet, the next morning he came in and did the same thing. Now I was fuming. It was one thing to do it and not know (because he could not read my mind), but to do it after I expressed how it made me feel…that was a bridge too far.

The next morning, I was ready. He came in, sat down, closed his eyes, and launched into his brief cereal-prayer. I took my bowl, extended my arm across the table, and held my bowl right under his nose. I mean, like millimeters under his nose. After what I'm assuming was his "amen moment," he opened his eyes to see my cereal so close that I now know Cheerios have no smell.

His head snapped back, and he about fell over backwards out of his chair. "What in the world?" He was really off-put by my prayer solution. I simply said that I thought our prayers over food should be out loud together, but if he wouldn't come to me on this issue, I would come to him. Thorderson thought it over for a minute, then nodded his head. He never did a silent prayer over his cereal again while we were together.

Those were our only two issues that I can recall…typical missionary conflicts. There is no doubt that living together with a missionary partner and learning how to deal with that dynamic presents the biggest growth challenge for young people serving in Church Missions around the world. Making a partnership work among the pettiness and the real challenges certainly prepares every missionary for future relationships with their spouse.

Thorderson and I were no different. It was a minor miracle we were so close considering that both of us were alpha males. Bottom line…Thordy made missionary work fun.

We were pals.

Thordy and his cereal.

Fart Therapy

> At age 4, Mom and Dad enrolled me in a Catholic pre-school. I do not remember it at all. My parents loved to tell a story about how I was asked at age 4 to write, direct and produce the Christmas play. According to legend, I immediately cast classmates into the starring roles of Jesus, Mary, and Joseph Smith.
>
> The nuns loved it.

Final Four

Another commonality was the love of basketball shared by Thorderson and me. We played one on one almost every P-day, and he destroyed me. I was average at best, and Thordy exposed how truly mediocre I was. He was headed to Wayne State in Michigan on a basketball scholarship after the Mission, so he was a legit player. I thought I was more than I was, and he showed me the true nature of my inability.

When March Madness rolled around in the Spring of 1987, we were going insane wanting to watch the games. Missionaries are supposed to focus 100% on the Work, so watching the games was out of the question, but the Final was on Monday, and that's our P-day…so…

We figured (stupidly) that the Lord knew this would happen when he put two basketball fanatics together. Our plan had been factored in.

We had thrifted a little TV and found a way to plug it into the cable line of the apartment underneath us. We ordered pizza and made popcorn. We sat and cheered feeling normal. For Thorderson, it was a peek back into the real world. He would complete his two years later that month and go back to basketball in Michigan.

We jumped around the apartment in disbelief when Derrick Coleman missed his free throws-leaving the door open for Keith Smart to hit that jumper from the left side-giving Indiana the win over Syracuse 74-73. We stayed on the game long enough to see the first airing of "One Shining Moment," now a standard element of March Madness.

We honestly did all that just to watch basketball, but later that week we peeked in on *Miami Vice*. The opening scene found Sonny in passionate lovemaking with some model. It was definitely not something two full-time missionaries should have been watching, so we frantically unhooked the cable and gave the TV to our neighbors. They were happy for the unexpected gift.

We did not tell them it was payment-in-kind for pirating their cable.

1987 March Madness

The following year, SIC Finance transferred my Dad to Las Cruces, New Mexico. We lived a short time in an apartment until they found a house on 1100 Mesilla in Old Town. They immediately enrolled me in Ms. Handy's Kindergarten, which is still there.

I have memories of learning to write there. I could look at whole passages of text, ten turn away from the book, and then copy down what I had read word for word.

We also had competitions on the playground using the swing to jump for distance. I hated losing, so I went for big air one day flying across the playground and hitting the slide...breaking my arm.

I won the jump challenge that day.

Hard-Headed

Would I ever learn?

Thordy and I were teaching a lady who had a son about five-years-old. We had a standing meeting three days a week at about 2:00 in the afternoon. She lived in an apartment complex that had long, dark hallways. When we visited her, one of us would stand down at the end of the hall holding the outside door open to provide light until the other found her door. As one of us would knock, the other would let the door to the outside close and run to catch up. There would be a brief moment of complete darkness in the hallway.

By the time the other hustled down the hall, her door would open and fill the hallway with light so we could see again. For two weeks we stopped by, taught her for an hour, and left. It was all very routine.

It came time to select a baptismal date and she told us that she would have to talk to her husband. She was worried because, "He's very Catholic and will not like this."

Cue the record scratch…your husband? It had been two weeks, and she had not mentioned anything about a husband. There were lots of pictures in the house, but none suggested a husband in the picture. All the photos of her son were of him alone or just the two of them. There were no mall shots with all three of them.

Two days after her revelation, we returned at our appointed time. I knocked and Thordy held the door down the hall providing light. After knocking, I heard the outside door close and knew Elder Thorderson was headed my way. A few seconds after the hall got dark, the apartment door opened. Normally the hall would fill with light from inside the apartment, but this time the door opened to a dark apartment with nothing but the soft glow from the TV inside the front room.

The back light revealed a silhouette in the doorway. I started to greet her by name and say, "It's us Elders." But before I could do so, I heard a man's voice ask in Spanish, "Are you the missionaries?" I nervously responded "Yes sir."

He said, "Good, I've got something for you."

As I was processing that, and thinking, "Wow, he made us cookies!" the door closed slightly as he reached for something behind it. Instantly I recognized the familiar rattle and tap of a shotgun being grabbed. Knowing that sound is a vital skill for any hillbilly. Nevertheless, time slowed down. I think my hillbilly brain and my missionary brain had a brief conversation. As the two sides discussed run vs. proselyte in slow motion, I became aware of a thumping sound. The sound of feet…Elder Thorderson's brain had no such conversation, and he was running at top speed, through the dark to the exit. He was smarter than me.

I heard the familiar cocking sound as I ran in hot pursuit of my companion. Thorderson was already out the door when I had a good 10-15 feet to go. I remember thinking, "He's going to fire that thing right now." The hall was again dark, and so to not give him a target, I fell into the stairwell just to the left of the exit door and bounded down two flights of dark stairs into a lobby of sorts, before running out the front doors of the apartment complex. I remember being afraid that the husband was running after me. He didn't.

Once outside, I really panicked, because in the chaos of the melee, Thordy and I had become separated. This was where things got dangerous for missionaries. I was also disoriented having taken a different route out of the apartment complex. So, I stopped, took a deep breath with my eyes closed, and re-centered myself. Suddenly, I could visualize where I was relative to where we usually entered the apartment complex. I started running again.

I ran to where we had parked our car to find Thorderson sitting in the driver's seat with the engine running. He looked very relieved that I made it out alive, and we sped off…never to return to that apartment. We never saw that lady again.

It's the last married woman I would ever teach without her husband.

To my dismay, the school called my Dad. He came barreling into the nurse's office and scolded me for claiming that my arm was broken. "If you're really not faking it, I'll take you to the doctor." I almost admitted to faking it, but I took a chance, and said that I wanted to go to the doctor. If it turned out to not be broken, I was a dead man. The X-ray showed a clean break, and I got my cast.

Later in life, my Mom told me it was the only time she saw my Dad cry. He never apologized to me directly.

Super Missionaries

The Gallegos family of Echo Park were the referral kings of the Arcadia Mission. We were at their house constantly eating great food and teaching the next round of friends and contacts they brought by. Seriously, I don't think there has ever been a more member-missionary focused family in the Church. We loved them dearly.

When Thorderson and I left the area, they cried.

After two years of kindergarten, I started first grade at Alameda Elementary. There I had my first "girlfriend," Cindy. I also wrote, directed, and produced my sophomore effort *This Is Your Life, Charlie Brown* casting myself in the lead role.

I drove my 2nd grade teacher so crazy that she gave me a piece of graph paper, a 12-inch ruler, a pencil, and an assignment to measure the entire school and draw it to scale on the single piece of graph paper.

It took me all year, but Ms. Jackson maintained her sanity.

The Ugliness

Sometimes things happened on my Mission that were tragic. I would like to say that the missionary experience was always neat, tidy and perfect; that everyone was just as advertised: smiling, happy, serving the Lord with full purpose of heart. To be fair - yes, it was mostly like that, but it was foolishness to think that any effort that big would be devoid of problems. During my time in Arcadia, there were approximately 30,000-40,000 missionaries worldwide. Currently there are over 90,000 full-time teaching or service missionaries.

I witnessed my fair share of internal strife. The Downs-Pearce fight was just the beginning. There were many sad stories in which I played a peripheral role. At the time, I just went about the work of dealing with whatever crisis came along. I didn't think a thing of it, but with decades of retrospect - I constantly wonder, "How in the world did I live through it all?" There was no way to predict all the craziness from the piney woods of East Texas.

One morning, my companion and I got a call to go to the Burbank airport. There was an Elder there we knew who had fled his apartment alone and was going home. He apparently had had sex with a member girl in a baptismal font filled with warm water at the Church, and he was now "out of here." He snuck out while his companion slept.

The mission rule was: if you did something so wrong that it would cause you to lose your membership in the Church, that action had to take place in the mission field prior to going home. We were the closest missionaries with a car to the airport, so the job fell to us to retrieve this Elder and deliver him to the mission office.

So, my companion and I headed to the airport and found the gate where we saw the Elder sitting nearby with a hat pulled down over his eyes. My companion and I sat down on both sides of him, and I told him that we were there to take him to see the Mission President. I assured him that after the meeting, we would bring him right back to the airport.

He refused to move. He wasn't a huge guy, but he was big enough. When he asked what happens if he refused to go, I told him that one way or another he was going with us. Quickly considering the impending fight, I was suddenly grateful for the inspiration to wear street clothes and not our missionary uniforms. Thinking quickly, I finally said, "Haven't you brought enough attention to yourself today? Come on, let's go meet with President Meier. You know he is a good man, and eventually, you are going to have to deal with this. Why not do it the right way?" He went with us. It was really sad. The rides to the mission home and back to the airport were completely silent except for the Elder softly weeping in the backseat. I can't get the vision or the sound out of my head…even three decades later.

Another time, my companion and I got a call to pick up a sister missionary who had tried to kill herself. She apparently had undiagnosed mental health issues that had erupted in the mission field. She tried to slit her wrists open, and her sister-companion missionary had saved her. Now she was going home. When we pulled the mission van up to her apartment, she came out with a blanket over her head which completely covered her from head to toe except for her eyes.

She got in the van with no luggage, and the blanket never moved. We drove her to LAX without a word. She got out and disappeared into the terminal alone with the blanket still over her head. We never saw her again. We drove her companion and a new sister back to their apartment. They were both traumatized. I think the Mission paid for therapy for the sisters who stayed so that they could continue their service.

There was another day when my companion and I decided to go visit Elders around the Zone as part of my leadership duties. We pulled up to one apartment on the ground floor and knocked, but no one answered. Funny thing: we could hear sounds of life and music coming from inside. They wouldn't open the door, even though they knew we were there.

There was an open window, so I knocked out the screen and crawled inside. These two knuckle-heads had a department store worth of stuff inside their apartment. They had TVs, VCRs, stereos, boom boxes, and Atari and Nintendo gaming consoles. What's more: they had joined numerous *16-cassettes-for-1-cent* clubs. That was a thing back in the day.

You joined a music club for a penny, got 16 (or so) cassettes to start out, but were then obligated to buy one cassette a month at full price for a year.

National Suicide Prevent

[122] These two had joined under different missionary names using different missionary apartment addresses. They collected all the cassettes for themselves with no intention of ever fulfilling the terms of the contract. When I busted through the window, they both looked up from the leather recliners they had bought like two stoners in a movie starring Seth Rogan and Matthew McConaughey. I never took my eyes off them as I reached back and opened the door for my companion. We looked around with amazement at this impressive inventory of contraband.

I took one of the Elders with me leaving my companion with the other, and we went to the mission home to get the mission van. Upon returning to their apartment, we loaded up all their loot and delivered it all back to the mission home. The Mission President was pretty upset, but instead of sending the two entrepreneurial Elders home, he gave them the option of surrendering all their ill-gotten purchases and staying to complete their Missions. If they wanted, they could take their stuff and go home. They chose to stay.

The two were separated on the spot, and the A.Ps figured out where to put them for an emergency transfer. My companion and I were tasked with taking them to their new areas and shuttling everyone around until the crisis was resolved. Over the course of that day, everyone involved looked at these two slackers with contemptuous disdain.

For over a year, their stuff took up half of the garage at the mission home. Elders leaving the Mission at the end of their two years were invited to go out and pick an item they liked to take home with them.

At the end of my two years, I got a nice chess set that went back with me to East Texas.

> Heading into 3rd grade, my Dad announced we were moving back to Alamogordo. He had been promoted to Branch Manager of SIC Finance there. I may have been sad to go, but getting me a new dog, who I named Willie, helped.
> 2413 Westminster would be our new home.

A Different Guy

Elder Ashworth was a different guy. Most missionaries were cut from the same cloth…naive, wholesome…a little corny. Not Ashworth. He had tattoos, rocked a mullet that went down below his collar, wore John Lennon shades, and drank near-Beer on Sundays while listening to the Raiders on the radio.

We met under weird circumstances. He came into the Mission while Thorderson and I were the Zone Leaders over the Pasadena area. We heard a new missionary had arrived in the area, and we went over to meet him. We decided, as a joke to introduce ourselves very formally with, "Hi, I'm Elder Thorderson, and this is Elder Dale. We're your Zone Leaders;" the part about our titles said in unison. We thought it was hilarious. Ashworth thought (he later told me) that we were the two biggest idiot-dorks he had ever met, and he almost punched us both in the face.

Once I picked him and his companion up to take them to a Ward activity. As he got in the car, I was prattling on about something and didn't realize that the car was still rolling forward slowly. He put one leg in the car, but his outside leg got tucked in behind him and ultimately under the back wheel. He calmly said (over whatever story I was telling), "Elder…the car is on my leg…Could you please stop…Do you think you could do that…Please." He said it so nonchalantly that it took all of us a beat or two to figure out that he was talking to us and that he was being serious. I quickly stopped and reversed the car off of his foot.

Another time, I called to talk to him about an impending transfer to El Monte, California:

"Can I talk to Elder Ashworth?"
"He's downstairs changing out his laundry," replied his goofy companion.
"I'll wait."
"Ok."
After 10 minutes of sitting on the phone, "Elder, go get your companion. I need to talk to him."
"Ok," said the goof, "I'll get him and we'll call you back."

After half an hour, I called back, and no one answered. I was frustrated, but they were both knuckleheads in my mind, so I let it go until the morning. When we finally talked later the following day, I let him know he was being transferred to El Monte. It was all routine…it did not occur to me there was anything strange going on.

Months later, Ashworth confessed that the night I called to talk to him, he was not changing out his laundry; instead, he had gone with another Elder (not his companion), named Maclean, to San Diego where he repossessed a motorcycle he had sold to a guy before his Mission. This person had stopped paying Ashworth, and he needed the money to finance his Mission, because his parents were not contributing. He and Maclean walked from Echo Park to downtown L.A.…which took hours, then hopped a Greyhound to Oceanside that arrived very late at night. Ashworth's plan was to take a city bus the remainder of the way to Escondido where the motorcycle was, but it was too late at night. So, they slept on a bench at the bus station until the next morning. They mounted city buses headed east to

Escondido riding it to the end of the line then they walked the rest of the way.

Once they arrived in Escondido, they found the open field where Ashworth's bike sat neglected. They hopped the fence, grabbed the bike, and wrestled it through weeds and underbrush back onto the road. Somehow, Ashworth got it started, and after filling it with gas, he and Maclean mounted the Honda 550 together without helmets and rode the three hours back up the 405 to Echo Park. He really must have needed the money.

People around the world are usually surprised and shocked to find out that not only are missionaries not paid, they pay to be there! Missionaries, their families, friends, or members of the Ward back home usually put up money to pay for the Mission.

The system of paying for a Mission is different now, but back then, each Mission had a different cost based on the average standard of living within the mission boundary. Arcadia, at that time, was about $400 per month. That money paid for an apartment and covered other mission costs such as utilities, phones, and cars. Parents usually deposited money directly into a missionary's bank account to cover other costs, such as food…but we ate a lot in member's homes, so my money went to clothes and books.

There was a certain noble rarity around the missionary who paid for their own Mission. It fit Ashley's brand that he himself paid. He was not beholden to anyone.

Ashworth quickly sold the bike to pay for a few more months of his Mission.

Now, I only came to know the full details of this crazy story long after my mission service. During our time serving together, Ashworth only intimated about going to San Diego to get the bike. I always assumed a member drove him and his companion down there with a flat-bed trailer to retrieve his property…which by the way is adequately rogue on its own. The actual story is beyond incredible for any LDS missionary. It is unheard of. The actual events are beyond epic…and reckless.

I asked him recently how he got Maclean to go. He said, "I just told him that I needed to go get a bike outside San Diego, and would he go with me." Ashworth said Maclean was the best guy and just agreed without knowing the full plan. Personally, I think Maclean, being from England, had no idea how far it was. Ashworth confirms this by sharing that the trip just unfolded in parts…the walk downtown…the Greyhound to Oceanside…the city buses to Escondido…sleeping outside on a bench…the ride back. All individually epic pieces that Maclean just accepted as they unfolded. What a wing-man!

This whole operation was entirely outside the lines of the mission rules…leaving his area, leaving his companion…shoot, leaving the Mission. Sleeping on a bench overnight?!? All these were really serious violations, and would probably have resulted in them both being sent home. But not Ashworth. He did things differently, and was headed to El Monte.

We would see each other again.

> By the 5th grade at Sierra Elementary, I was in Mr. Wilson's class. Charlie Ashcroft (no relation to Elder Ashcroft) was my best friend, and we co-lead a crew that included Sam Fambrough, Randy Brown, and Orlando Cisneros. I had two "girlfriends" there: twins, Jan and June. They worked in the cafeteria, and we would brush hands when they handed me my lunch tray. Just their touch sent electricity through me from head to toe. Not understanding the religious irony at such a young age, I would lay in bed at night, and imagine being married...to both of them.

A Sign

Around the last week of Thorderson's time in the Mission, he admitted to me that he had never seen the beach. I grew up in South Texas, so I had frequently been to the beaches on the Gulf Coast. There had also been a couple of body-boarding trips to San Diego with my cousins.

I was blown away to meet someone who had never seen the ocean in person and up close, so I suggested we go. Echo Park was just a few miles up the 10 freeway from Santa Monica; though with mission rules prohibiting travel outside the area, it seemed like a lifetime away.

Nonetheless, we jumped on the freeway and headed west on a clear and sunny Southern California day. Not a cloud in the sky. We were both feeling more than a little guilty, but having Thorderson see the ocean seemed worth it. I felt like I was facilitating a Make-a-Wish moment...minus the cancer. Also worth mentioning: missionaries were forbidden to swim...ever. Getting in the water was a big no-no. So, we were going just to stand on the beach for Thorderson to see the Pacific. Lame, but we were young.

[128] As we crossed the 405, suddenly it became overcast. The clouds increased to the point that by the time we exited the 10 in Santa Monica, visibility was close to zero. We couldn't even see the sand from Pacific Coast Highway. It was a cloudy, foggy, and blustering day. We decided to quickly turn around and get back to the Arcadia Mission boundaries.

Back in our Echo Park apartment, we could not decide if the weather was some sort of beach phenomenon or a sign from God that we had crossed a line…literally.

It wasn't until later in life, while living in Redondo Beach and Manhattan Beach, that I learned about marine layer. It can be a cloudless sunny day in downtown L.A. but completely overcast at the beach. Neither downtown nor the beach has any idea of the sun or the clouds being experienced by the other. Many *June-gloom* mornings on a cloudy beach day, I would sit in the sand…reminiscing on Thorderson and me freaking out over the clouds God had sent to punish us for wanting to see the beach outside of our assigned mission area…and laugh.

Thorderson went home without seeing the Pacific.

There was a pencil machine next to the bathrooms at Sierra Elementary. For two years, it would spit out a Ticonderoga No. 2 if you pushed two dimes into the slot like a coin operated washing machine. In the fall of my 5th grade year, they stocked the machine with pencils showing NFL colors and team names.

I was addicted to NFL football, so I started buying all the pencils I could. This would be my first foray into business.

Attwooll

In April of 1987, after only a year in the Arcadia Mission, I got the call that I would be following Thorderson as the leader of Zone 7. I suppose I saw it coming, but what I did not predict was the assignment of my new companion, Elder Attwooll.

I had cut his hair prior to our companionship, so I knew some things about him. If the Arcadia Mission had been illustrated by Charles Schultz, Attwooll would have been Pigpen. As a notorious neat-freak and hyper-sensitive to hygiene, I was nervous about him joining me. Thorderson was a neat-freak like me, so the apartment had a certain sanitized vibe to it when Attwooll arrived.

On the day of transfers, Attwooll showed up with nothing but a garbage bag.

He sat down on the bed that had been occupied by Thordy the night before. I asked what was in the bag, and he said, "My clothes" - like *duh what else would it be?* Where was all the rest of his stuff? His belongings? He just sat there and said, "My bike is outside, but this is all my stuff."

Missionaries do not have a lot of stuff, but over the course of the Mission, you accumulate things. Clothes, books, photos and souvenir knick-knacks are the norm. I had some possessions by that point in the Mission, but missionaries travel light. After two years, I had to mail home two large moving boxes.

Attwooll had a garbage bag.

I took a deep cleansing breath, pulled a dining chair close to him and said, "Ok..." another deep breath to stay calm... "I like things clean. So, you use a dish, clean it. Done with your clothes? Put them in a laundry bag. Wash your sheets weekly. Bathe every night." I paused to see if this was sinking in or getting through. He looked at me dead-pan, without blinking and said, "For me, it can have an inch of dirt on it, and I'll eat it."

Holy cow.

As he sat there, he was in his missionary uniform...white shirt, dark tie, dark pants, missionary tag, and very worn shoes. Most missionaries keep it looking as nice as they can, but Attwooll's missionary uniform looked like he had wrestled a bobcat...on a dirt mat...in a very small space.

"Ok, so how much money do you have?" That's what came out of my mouth. He said that he had about $150. So, I thought we might be in business. "Let's look at your bike." It was decent, so we loaded it up on the back of our mission car and headed to the mission home. The new missionaries were coming in that day; there were going to be customers. He got another $150 for the bike.

We headed to my favorite thrift haunts and picked up two new suits, five pairs of pants, a dozen white shirts, and ties. We found three new pairs of shoes, a dozen pairs of socks, and a couple of sweaters and belts. At the end, he still had $100 left, so we picked him up some groceries, all new hygiene items, wash cloths, and towels. I had two sets of sheets, so I gave him one, and he bought a new pillow.

When we got back to our apartment, a "pad" in mission lingo, I cut his hair. He had really bad acne, so I made a batch of paste out of shampoo and salt that he applied like a mask. I bought him an electric razor, because he would have bled to death from a blade. That first day with Attwooll was one for the ages.

After about two weeks, his face cleared up completely, and he looked like a million bucks. We had a baptism that day, so there were pictures. Apparently, he sent the photo home to his parents in his weekly letter.

After about three weeks together, our apartment phone rang one Sunday night. I answered, and a female voice said, "Elder Dale, this is Sister Attwooll. I am Elder Attwooll's Mom. I just saw a photo of him, and I cannot believe how healthy he looks. I called the Mission President, who told me what you have done to get him looking so good. I got permission to call and thank you. You have no idea how comforting it is to know how well he is doing. Thank you so much."

Caught completely off-guard and not knowing what to say, I managed a, "Thank you ma'am. Would you like to talk to Elder Attwooll?" She declined saying that she did not have permission to talk to him, just me. Hilarious now looking back, but at the time, I took it in stride. I just repeated "ok, and thank you again." We eventually hung up.

It felt weird being thanked for what I had done. I only did it because there was no way Pigpen and Schroeder were ever going to make it together. Elder Attwooll and I got along well. How could you not like him? He was a harmless teddy bear.

[132] We were together for three months before we both got transferred out of Del Rio. Merely a month later, we saw each other again at a mission conference. He came in looking like he had been run over by a garbage truck. His pants had an odd look to them, and at close glance I discovered he had stapled them up the length of the outside seam. What the heck? "I tore them riding a bike, so I just stapled them up...good as new."

I just sighed and shook my head. He was somebody else's problem now.

My first real memory in life, other than still pictures set as memories, was Super Bowl V. I was 4-years old. The Dallas Cowboys had finally got past the NFC Championship game, and they faced the Baltimore Colts. The Cowboys dominated the game until a 4th quarter comeback threatened the whole thing. In an iconic moment, tight end, and back-up kicker O'Brien, hit a chin-strap-dangling 32-yard field goal as time expired to give Baltimore the win.

My father, a rabid Cowboys fan, jumped up from the recliner we were sharing, yelled a not-good out-loud word, and kicked out the front of our TV set with his pointed-toe boot.

I was a Cowboy fan for life.

Close Call

Attwooll and I had been teaching Rogelio for a couple of weeks. His wife was a member, and they had a couple of kids under the age of eight. Rogelio had promise, because his brother was a Bishop in Guatemala; it seemed everyone had a brother who was a Bishop in Guatemala. Rogelio came to Church the first week we taught him but not the second week.

When we finally caught up to him to find out why, he told Elder Attwooll and me that he didn't see the point in getting baptized into the Mormon church, and unless God gave him a sign, he wouldn't join. I asked him what he meant by "a sign," and he replied, "nothing fancy, just a clear answer." We said that we would be back in two days, and that that would be exactly what would happen. I would later wonder what *nothing fancy* vs. *fancy* looks like in this context.

For the next 48 hours, Attwooll and I studied and prayed fervently to know what to do. We had heard of a bold strategy from some other Elders: instruct the person to start the prayer, telling God, "I'm going to kneel here until I get an answer." That sounded risky to me, and it sounded like a gamble whose price would be some sore knees. Nonetheless, we determined this to be our course of action with Rogelio.

To clarify a point of doctrine: it is not the practice of members of The Church of Jesus Christ of Latter-day Saints to ask for a sign from God. It is considered bad form, at best, with the petitioner provoking God into a negative reaction. There is a Book of Mormon story in Alma 30 of a man named Korihor who asked the prophet Alma for a sign. In short: it ended poorly for Korihor.

So, the fact that we were even entertaining the idea of participating in the petitioning of a sign was unusual, and not the least bit reckless. In retrospect, I think I would have done just about anything to get someone into the waters of baptism.

When we got to Rogelio's house and were seated, I said, "Rogelio, do you really want to know from God what you should do?"
"Yes."
"Rogelio, are you willing to put in the effort, and do whatever it takes to get an answer from God." Thinking a moment, he then looked straight at me, "Yes."

"Ok," I immediately jumped into action, "Here is what you are going to do. We'll all kneel with you and you give a prayer that simply says, 'Heavenly Father, I want to know if this is your Church and if I should be baptized.' Then stop talking and do not end the prayer with 'in the name of Jesus Christ, Amen' until you get the answer from Him. Got it?"
"You mean, kneel there quietly on my knees after I ask until I get an answer?"
"Yep."

After a moment, he slowly and timidly moved off the couch on to his knees, and so did we.

"Heavenly Father," he said almost imperceptibly, "I want to know if this is all the truth, and if I should get baptized by these Elders." *Not the same, but close enough*, I thought. He then stopped talking. We were there, the three of us, on our knees, silently waiting for Rogelio to get his answer.

For my part, I had never prayed so hard in my life. I was imploring, no, begging God to please answer him. "Make him feel something that will convince him that he has received an answer from on High." The silence went on for an immeasurable amount of time. If you have never tested this scenario, stand quietly in front of a group of people and time the silence. What seems forever is more like 10 seconds. This silence probably went on for a minute, but it seemed like an eternity. Then Rogelio quietly muttered, "In the name of Jesus Christ, Amen."

We all looked up. Across the room from us, Rogelio sat maybe 8 feet away. He looked ashen. I said, "Well, did you get your answer? "
"Yes," he replied quietly, "but you didn't have to hit me."
"Huh?," I said, not knowing if he was joking or serious.
"Yeah." Again, he looked scared. "I felt this burden lifted from my shoulders, then one of you slapped me. I opened my eyes and ended the prayer, but you both are all the way over there. What's going on?"
"Rogelio, neither one of us hit you. I don't know what that was."
"It was God," his eyes were very wide.

I had seen a lot in the mission field by this point, but that seemed strange to me too. Hey, whatever it takes…I pressed on, "So what do you want to do?"
"Get baptized," he was very sincere.
Right at that moment, his wife entered the living room, "*Gordo*, your brother is on the phone." He got up and went to the kitchen while we updated his tearful and grateful wife.

After a few minutes, Rogelio emerged from the kitchen. Without a word to any of us, he turned down the hallway with a determined look. Startled, we all stood, and I looked down the hallway where Rogelio was with his back to me in the master bedroom. As I walked toward him, he started brushing his hair. Strangely, he applied Chapstick. At the time it meant nothing to me, but later it was a detail that haunted me.

When I entered the master bedroom, he saw me and spun on his heel before walking to his bed and sitting down. Now, this master bedroom was of the old tradition: two single beds with enough space in between them to sit facing each other with your legs in the middle. It was a small room, so this was likely the most efficient way to have enough bed for both spouses.

I sat on the other bed facing him. I didn't even realize that I had left Attwooll in the living room with Rogelio's wife and kids. We were alone. The beds were so close that we had to odd/even our leg placement. He looked like a ghost.
"Rogelio, what is it?"
"The phone call was my brother…my Dad just died."
"I'm so sorry Rogelio, how old was h—"
"No," he interrupted, "this is all my fault. I asked for a sign. You warned me not to ask God for a sign, and you were right. I should not have tempted God. I killed my father."

I sat there speechless…mouth-breathing, not knowing what to say as he flung himself prostrate on the bed sobbing uncontrollably.

As I leaned in to touch his leg and reassure him, I failed to understand that he didn't fling himself on the bed for dramatic effect; he was reaching for something. For a second my mind registered the tell-tale "clank" of heavy metal. Before I could react, he swung back up with a big gun in his hand. It later turned out to be a .38, but when it's pressed between your eyes…literally the little spot between my two eyes. The barrel of the gun looked HUGE. He pressed the gun against my head while sobbing out of control.

Our eyes met, and his registered nothing.

Death.

Before I could react at all, he moved the gun away from my head and put it up to the side of his own head. Again, I was still frozen, but this all happened very fast. My mind was still trying to dislodge the "What in the heck is happening" question. Luckily, my brain kicked into gear simultaneously with him second-guessing the gun placement.

He muttered, "Not here," and as he was moving the gun from the side of his head to under his chin, I pounced. I threw both my hands against the side of his gun-hand resulting in the two of us falling onto his bed. The gun, his hand, and both my hands pressed up and away. Problem was: all that mess of hands and gun disappeared under the stacks of pillows on the bed. I screamed in Spanish for him to let go of the gun. I had him fairly well pinned, and I was 100 pounds heavier. After I demanded a few times, he muttered, "Ok," and I slowly started pulling his arm from under the pillow.

I saw the muzzle first. He had flexed his wrist and turned the barrel. Before I could think of what to do, his finger snapped at the trigger, but his hand placement was bad, and he missed. That he attempted to fire the pistol really pissed me off. Something in me snapped, and while I held his arm with one hand, I arched my back to get separation and started punching him in the side of his head as hard and as fast as I could. It was violent and shocking. The first blows closed his eyes, but I gave him a few more for good measure, and he relaxed. I put my elbow on the side of his head and threw away the pillows with my other hand, all while still holding on to his gun arm.

Removing the pillows revealed that he had let go of the gun.

He was unconscious, but breathing. I grabbed the gun and put it under the waist band in the back of my pants covering it with my suit coat. I left him there, which was dumb. People who have one gun usually have two, but I was reeling mentally…and new at this game of disarming homicide/suicides. The thought that ran through my head at top speed was: "He really wanted to shoot me!"

When I came into the living room, Attwooll was sitting on the floor playing jacks with the kids. For some reason that angered me even more; fat, dumb, and happy as usual while I'm in the other room about to die. I walked by him and without stopping, slapped him hard on the back of the head, "Get up, come with me. You, too," as I pointed at Rogelio's wife.

They had a long driveway, and I walked the length of it with a purpose. When we got to the gate, Rogelio's wife said, "Elder, what's the matter?"

"This!" I yelled pulling the gun from my waistband. "Oh, fetch," gasped Attwooll. He couldn't even cuss right.

"Yeah." I popped open the cylinder, ejected the shells into my coat pocket, and handed the empty gun to Rogelio's wife. That was my second dumb move. The gun should have never gone back into the house of a suicidal person. Again, I was doing the best I could in the moment.

I relayed to Rogelio's terror-stricken wife all that had happened. When I got to the part where I knocked him out, she turned and ran screaming back into the house. Sure, it's not every day that Mormon missionaries knock your husband unconscious, so I wasn't offended that there were no good-byes. I never saw either of them again.

After having been nearly shot so many times, I finally called and told the Mission President. To be frank, I now know that I called him because for the first time on the Mission, I was genuinely shaken up by what had happened. It was close up; it was personal, and I had come out of it miraculously lucky.

President Meier instructed me to turn Rogelio over to the Stake Missionaries (locally appointed members who do missionary work). He also called the Stake President in the area to say that if Rogelio ever came to church, it needed to be to a Ward where I was not serving, and to inform him that Rogelio had a predilection for gun play.

President Meier asked if I wanted to transfer out of the area, and I told him no. That's not my style, really.

There was no mention of Attwooll in any of the conversations. Guess he was expendable. I know that's not true, but I still find it funny.

> At 11-years-old with no job, my discretionary budget was no match for my insatiable urge to buy more NFL football pencils. So, every Monday, I took my Mom's check for $5, bought a week's worth of lunch tickets, then resold them for face value to kids who, let's say, had a body type that required more than one lunch tray. I converted the cash into dimes at a convenience store, the PicQuik near my house and then bought more pencils on Tuesday.
>
> As an adult, I am painfully aware that I was laundering money. Soon, I had bought out the entire pencil machine.

Planting Seeds

Remember Sister Pearce? The knife-wielding Brit who took exception to her companion not wanting to get out of the car in the rain up in La Crescenta? Well, she got transferred to Burbank around the same time I became the leader of Zone 7. I don't think she liked me too much, and I was too mule-headed to do anything about it.

Though I had my chances...

For example, she called one evening very excited that she and her companion had placed a Book of Mormon in every room of the twin Marriotts off Olive and the 5 Freeway.

She was so happy that they had accomplished such a thing. I probably would have just moved along, but when she said, "Elder, we planted so many seeds today," I was like a dog with a bone: I couldn't just pass it by.

All I had to do…all I had to do was say, "That's great Sister Pearce, good job." It would have been so easy. To this day I laugh at my inability just to take the easy road. Yeah, no.

Instead, I calmly requested, "Read section 4 of the Doctrine and Covenants, and call me back." What an idiot, what's wrong with me?

You see, Section 4 famously declares:

> Behold the field is white already to harvest; and lo, he that thrusteth in his sickle with his might, the same layeth up in store that he perisheth not, but bringeth salvation to his soul."

In other words, *this is not a time to be planting seeds. This is a time to harvest!* By this time, my various companions and I had a mission-wide reputation of being baptizers…finishers. Think Alec Baldwin, who was sent here by Mitch and Murray from Downtown. I'd love to say I was channeling Blake years ahead of the movie, but no.

My *Idiot's Hall of Fame of Leadership* request that Sister Pearce read Section 4 was only met by silence on the other end of the phone, then a click. My only solace was that Attwooll thought it was the most gangster thing he had ever heard. He even tried to high five me. His approval did not shield me from the blow back.

Zone 7 had more Sister companionships than all the other ten zones combined. With Burbank and Pasadena in the Zone, the areas were not quite as rough as other places. President Meier preferred to assign females to safer areas so we had more than our share of Sister companionships. It also meant we had more cars in our Zone than any of the other Zones. In that era, Sisters never rode bikes. I hear it happens now, which is great, but I have never personally seen it.

The issue with having so many Sisters is that I was

outnumbered in the event that I caused an offense, and I had. Sister Pearce mounted a rebellion, of sorts. Each week, every missionary had to write a letter to the Mission President reviewing the work done: talking about people they were teaching, asking for assistance or resources if needed, and discussing any struggles they were having personal or otherwise.

For the next few months, every Sister in every weekly letter signed her name then wrote "…and as for Elder Dale, D&C 121:45." That verse reads," We have learned by sad experience that it is the nature and disposition of almost all men, as soon as they get a little authority, as they suppose, they will immediately begin to exercise unrighteous dominion."

In an era before the coinage of the term "clapback," it was the ultimate clapback.

They were basically saying that I was an unfit, unrighteous, abusive, bad leader, who was misusing his position of authority. It was hard to argue that I hadn't done something dumb, so I suppose I deserved it. I wish I could say now that I learned a lesson then that would serve me well in life, but instead I recognize it was the first in a long string of lessons on how to not be so aggressively idiotic.

It did subside some after President Meier organized a Zone meeting just for the Sisters, me, and Attwooll in the Glendale Stake Center. President Meier opened the meeting and then allowed an open forum for anyone in the Zone to get up and air a grievance. It was a feeding frenzy by the 20-25 Sister missionaries in attendance. They said awful things about me. I just sat there. After about 30-45 minutes of it, he thanked them for their feedback and closed the meeting.

As I sat there stunned that I was not allowed to say anything, even the apology I had loaded up, he turned, leaned down, and whispered, "Come on, let's go get some pancakes."

He took Attwooll and me to breakfast with the A.P.s where he explained that the Sisters needed to unload their frustrations and be heard. He described it as a pressure relief valve. There was no need to engage. He advised me to be more careful with my words, love and support those whom I lead, and let the whole thing be of good experience.

President Meier said, "You have a long life of leadership ahead of you. Never forget this. You screw up? You take your medicine and move on." THAT lesson has stayed with me.

I loved President Meier.

Word was out across campus that I had pencils for sale. There were two types of customers: fellow collectors and kids who just needed a pencil. So, I set up shop in the shade near the monkey bars. I had the pencils wrapped together in a big rubber band that created a circle of pencils the circumference of a No. 10 can. Once on the playground, I laid them out on a towel grouped by team. I noticed that I had more of some teams than others. And by that time, I had numerous complete sets of the then 28-team league.

Never Get Out of the Boat

It was a Monday night. Attwooll and I were winding down after a busy day when the apartment phone rang.

I answered it to hear Sister Brown in a panic. She was calling from a pay phone down on Figueroa Street, because their car had broken down. When I asked where she was exactly, she answered, "Well I'm on the corner of 39th and Fig."

Thinking it through, I asked her to go into a restaurant I knew to be right by her. To that she responded, "What about my companion?"

Um...she should go into the restaurant too, right?

It turns out that the two of them decided that one needed to stay with the car in case someone came to help, and the other should go call me and Attwooll. I never got to the bottom of who they thought was going to just miraculously stop by.

I may have raised my voice just a little when I suggested that she get back to her companion with all due haste. "Where's the car?" I asked, now standing in our apartment.

"It's on 45th and Fig," was the answer. I barely heard it. Holy cow, it was almost 9:00pm. This is a bad situation. You see, Figueroa Street was (and still is) dangerous. No one just goes down there at night unless they have a reason. Drive-by shootings and other violence were a weekly, if not daily, occurrence in the late 1980s.

This was bad, and they were really separated.

Remembering how poorly I had recently reacted to Sister Pearce, I gathered myself. Though, I suggested something I never would otherwise: I advised Sister Brown to go into the restaurant alone and wait for us. "You mean be separated from my companion?" Taking a deep breath, I let her question go instead of yelling into the phone: "That train has sailed!" - a twisted up euphemism from my Dad.

Instead, I calmly said that it would not be long, and we would pick her up. We quickly called Elder Graebel before squealing our tires in hot pursuit.

About 10 minutes later, we picked up Sister Brown and arrived at their car to find her companion safely inside. From the experience in La Crescenta, I should have remembered Sister Downs commitment to not getting out of the car. It paid off in this crisis.

Elder Graebel and his companion pulled up about the same time as we did. Graebel threw the keys to his car to Sister Brown, grabbed his toolbox, and told everyone to go home. Later I heard he got the car started, worked on it a few days, then returned it good as new to the Sisters. What a beast.

Missionaries should always stick together and never be apart…period. Yes, I had seen *Apocalypse Now* prior to my

Mission. So, at our next District Leader meeting, without referencing the incident or the movie, I asked them all to reiterate to the missionaries in their districts: "Never get out of the boat. Stay together!"

The other lesson I learned from this situation is: no matter how much the people in your organization might be mad at you, they still know you will come running in a crisis…if you have made it clear that you will in fact come running, no matter what they say about you.

Baptisms in Del Rio Branch (Echo Park)

Date	Name of Person	Baptized by:
8 Feb 87	Irene Sainz	Thorderson
8 Feb 87	Melva La Cayo	Thorderson
8 Feb 87	Maria La Cayo	Thorderson
8 Feb 87	Judith La Cayo	me
8 Feb 87	Marta Adilia La Cayo	me
8 Feb 87	Walter Jose Picado	me
15 Feb 87	Rosa Delia Ortiz	Thorderson
15 Feb 87	José Noé Ortiz	Thorderson
22 Feb 87	Maria Leticia Rivas	me
22 Feb 87	Selene Nicte Arqueta	me
22 Feb 87	Irma Celeste Herrera	me
22 Feb 87	Alan Daniel Arqueta	Thorderson
22 Feb 87	Maria de Carmen Garcia	Thorderson
22 Feb 87	Adan Gutierrez	Thorderson
1 Mar 87	Marta Morales	Thorderson
12 Apr 87	Luis Galeas	Wm.Pastrán
21 Apr 87	Angela Victoria Araujo	Thorderson
26 Apr 87	Aníbal Morales	me
17 May 87	Reina Aguilar	me
17 May 87	Manuela Sillas	Attwooll
17 May 87	William Walter Roman	me
7 Jun 87	John Jairo Lopez Noboa	Attwooll

I had a bunch of the newly formed Seahawks and Buccaneers pencils along with Lions, Patriots, and Saints. I only had a few Cowboys, Steelers, Raiders, and Rams. So, I set up price points based on quantity. If you wanted a pencil that I had many of, I would charge 20 cents. A Cowboys, Steelers, Raiders, and Rams pencil was $2 dollars.

By the time the school figured out the machine was empty and refilled it, I had enough revenue to buy out the machine in one shot the same day. I was the king of pencils at Sierra Elementary School.

Same Old Song and Dance

It would be my final transfer, but for the first time, my companion would stay. Attwooll welcomed a new Zone Leader (whose name I cannot recall), and I was going to be a Zone Leader in El Monte, which was on the other side of the Mission. I had served for 11 months in the San Fernando Valley, and now I was going to the San Gabriel Valley for the first time. For about a minute, I was looking forward to serving in another Zone besides Zone 7, but in the transfer phone call the A.P.s told me the zones were being realigned and renumbered. I was the new leader of Zone 7…in El Monte.

Upon arrival, I got a list of names, addresses, and phone numbers of the District Leaders serving in the Zone from the A.P.s. The third name they read-off to me was Elder DeFiguerido, who had just been called to serve in his first leadership posting.

It was late on a Monday. I loaded up my new companion, Elder

Buchanan, and headed over to DeFiguerido's pad. When we arrived, and found him there, I greeted him warmly before asking his companion to step outside with my companion. It had been around six months since we had served together, and I had changed during that time.

I worked more maturely and deliberately. I was not such a hyper-active stress case to everyone around me. I knew things. I had experience.

This increased maturity helped me realize that how I treated DeFiguerido was completely unnecessary…even inappropriate at times; like marking off days on his going-home-to-get-married calendar while he was drugged out from getting his wisdom teeth removed, causing him to lose a week of time. The pen he used had pink glitter ink so give me a break! Still, it was wrong.

We sat down together in the kitchen to talk. He looked great: crisp white shirt, polished shoes, and he had lost a bunch of weight - in a healthy way. I took a deep breath and started to sincerely apologize for everything.

He stopped me quickly and said something I'll never forget, "Don't you dare apologize to me. You were exactly what I needed. When I arrived in the Mission, I was soft. You did not coddle me. You made me strong. You showed me how to work." I was, at that point, tearing up as he was going on. "You showed me how to find, teach, and baptize. You helped me understand that the process is not a mystery. It's not working hard; it's doing the right work. I don't know if you've noticed, but I have been the top baptizing English Elder for the past six months."

I had noticed.

Aerosmith

[152] Now completely emotional and thankful for his forgiveness, I just hugged him. "Thank you," I managed, "You have no idea how bad I've been feeling."

"Well," he smiled, "I don't think you do anything half way."

I'm sure someone complained. One day the principal, Mr. McNeeley came over the P.A. in my class. "Mr. Dale, please come to my office and bring your pencils." Crap...I headed out with my pencils to the chorus of "oooooooohs" one gets when summoned to the principal's office.

Once in his office, he notified me that my father was on the way, and that my days as the pencil-Corleone of the playground were over. I sat quietly until my Dad walked in...sure that I was once again a dead man.

President Coleman

President Meier transferred me to El Monte then went home. He and his wonderful wife had completed their three-year Mission, and he was headed back to Salt Lake to his famous "Meier's Fine Foods" meat business. He was probably in his late 60s, so I'm sure he was ready to slow down. He and Sister Meier were incredible people, and I loved them dearly.

So, as Santa and Mrs. Claus got on the plane, Mr. and Mrs. CEO got off the plane. President and Sister Coleman were younger, I would guess in their early 50s at the time. They were fit and good-looking. They wore expensive suits and had kids younger than we were. They could not have been more different than President and Sister Meier.

I did not like the situation one bit. President Coleman was a big-shot in the Church Education System, which meant he had spent his life teaching early morning Seminary to high school

Meier's Meats and Fine Foods

students and Institute of Religion classes to college students. He had about-to-be-a-General-Authority written all over him, and revolutionizing missionary work in Arcadia was going to be the next step in him making his mark among Church leadership.

We clashed immediately.

President Coleman's first order of business was to release the A.P.s, all the Zone Leaders, and most of the District Leaders. Later in life, I would recognize the strategy of getting your own team in place, but at that time the move had a seismic effect on the Mission…and on me. He made a mistake of saying, in a meeting of new leadership, "Once we replace all of Meier's boys, we can do some real work." He said it in jest, but as the only "Meier's boy" in the room, I was the lone stoic among the delighted new blood; and of course, they thought President Coleman's comment was insightful, inspired, and hilarious.

In one of our subsequent one-on-one meetings together, I asked him why he kept me on as a Zone Leader…it seemed that he clearly did not like me. He responded, "Because you were the only one who didn't just tell me what I wanted to hear. You did not kiss up to me. You told me the brutal truth of the state of things. I knew right away I could depend on you for the unvarnished view." I took that lesson - of the importance speaking truth to power, through the remainder of my professional life.

The Arcadia Mission averaged about 150 baptisms per month, during the time of President and Sister Meier, which was very very good. By the time I left my Mission, nine months into President and Sister Coleman's time, we were up to about 300 per month. So, say what you want about the nurture vs. non-nurture differences between the two leadership styles, but President Coleman's way worked.

Also, President Coleman never moved me from El Monte. I would stay there nine months. That's a long time. Again, before

I left, I asked him why he never moved me. He said that he needed his most senior Zone Leader near the Los Angeles airport and the mission home.

But he never called me as one of his Assistants to the President (A.P.)…I took that hard.

Back in those days, being an A.P. meant you were the best of the best. You were destined for great things in the Church. You were "enough." If not, you were somehow less than. It took me years to get past it. Thankfully, this is not part of Church culture anymore.

I would be a Zone Leader for half of my time in Arcadia!

My Dad sat quietly as Mr. McNeely explained the entire operation. He had really done his reconnaissance well. He knew about the money laundering, how I had cornered the market, the price gouging, my market manipulation…everything. I really thought, "This was how I leave this world, and shed these mortal coils."

Mr. McNeely's pride faded when my Dad said, "You called me down here for this?" Dad hated coming to school.

Buchanan

When I arrived in El Monte, Elder Buchanan greeted me warmly. We had been in the MTC together but had served in completely separate areas. We saw each other at all-mission activities, such as the Christmas party or Mormon Night at Dodger Stadium. It was cool to see him again and serve with him, but we were the same age in the Mission. It took some adjustment for him to be junior to me as the Assistant Zone Leader, but he is the best guy you can imagine, so it was pretty chill.

Buchanan had only been in the area for a short time, but knew the lay of the land. We got along great. He was a good dude. He pointed out the important things to know about our apartment. First, there was an avocado tree right outside our front door on the second floor. When I arrived, they were nearly be ready to pick and eat, so guacamole was a staple there.

Secondly, the apartment had two full-size refrigerators. One was for our use, but the other had quit working a long time ago…no one knew exactly when… and it was sealed shut with

Mormon Night at Dodger Stadium

a bungee cord that wrapped all the way around it. He warned that some Elders a while back had opened it; the smell was so bad, it took weeks to get it out of the place.

Thirdly, the late-teenage boy downstairs was a bit of a player and every morning after his Mom went to work, he had loud sex with any number of various girls who would come around. That wasn't a problem for us…we were out of the apartment by 9-9:30 during the week…but on Sundays and Mondays, we would have to leave and get out of the place; it was so crazy down there.

Lastly, the El Monte apartment had a Sparkletts water dispenser! Like one of those you find in the break room of a bank or law office. Buchanan said a member paid for the service, and it was nice to always have a cold, fresh glass of water at any time, day or night.

About a week into my time in El Monte, I walked by the bathroom only to catch one of the English Elders filling up the blue Sparkletts bottle in the bath tub. When he saw me, he just looked away innocently, like nothing untoward was going on. I turned back to see Buchanan and the other English Elder cracking up.

They got me good.

It had been a running joke/welcome to the El Monte pad for a long time. We successfully pulled it on every new Elder over my next nine months there.

> Apparently, the pencil crisis had caused chaos and tears on the campus. I told Charlie that it was a mistake to put Sam in charge of security. He was huge! According to Mr. McNeely, kids were afraid to come over and purchase from us. They just went pencil-less. My daily sales records showed otherwise, but I knew better than to speak. It was my Dad's meeting.
>
> "Well," he told Mr. McNeely, "You're free to buy them back, I reckon."

The Right Stuff

The new El Monte version of Zone 7 was struggling. The standard metric of success at that time, baptisms, was down. The mission average per month by Zone was approximately fifteen. A good month in the Zone was upwards of twenty, and a bad month was below ten. Zone 7 had been clocking around six per month for a while when I arrived.

Part of the issue: there were far more English areas than Spanish in this particular Zone, and the English areas were predominately affluent. Traditionally, Spanish areas baptize more than English and less affluent areas are more successful. Nonetheless, the low numbers were disconcerting.

I was determined to show Elder Coleman that *Meier's boys* still had some fight in them.

Buchanan and I discussed it, and we decided to have a "morale day" in the Zone. We wanted to do it on a day other than Monday as that was the day missionaries did all their personal errands…shopping, cleaning, laundry, letter writing, haircuts, car maintenance, and such.

So, we picked out a Saturday and called all the missionaries in the Zone to meet us at the Stake Center in Hacienda Heights. The fact that they all had nothing better to do was not lost on me. We packed ourselves into the library there, and I passed out freshly popped popcorn, ice cold Cokes, and peanut M&Ms.

After a prayer, I told them that I thought they needed to relax and recharge. I had rented the movie *The Right Stuff*, and we were going to watch it. They all clapped and settled into lawn chairs and bean bags that I had borrowed from various members.

We watched the movie and thoroughly enjoyed ourselves. No training. No message. No stats. No challenges. Just relax. It seems silly in retrospect, but we just needed a little taste of normalcy…a sense of home.

When we arrived back at the pad in El Monte, I had a message from Branham giving me a heads up that President Coleman was not happy that we had spent the day watching movies and not working. I appreciated the heads up and even let it go that someone in the Zone ratted me out.

I didn't care…I believed in what we did.

Later that evening, President Coleman called. I thought about calling him first and confessing, but frankly, I was not sorry, and my Gram taught me to never apologize unless you are actually sorry.

When he asked if there was anything I needed to tell him, I responded "no;" he obviously already knew.

What a smart-aleck I was. He expressed his displeasure and disappointment to which I boldly asked him to watch the results before judging. *Let the ends judge the means*, right?

¹⁶⁰ Zone 7 led the Mission in baptisms for the next several months.

The Right Stuff

Mr. McNeely, the consummate professional, was one step ahead and had pulled from petty cash to buy me out. I was ready to take the money and run when Dad said, "Wait... son, Mr. McNeely is giving you back 20 cents per pencil. Is that what they're worth?"

"No sir," I said quietly, still thinking this could turn against me at any moment. "Well," Dad winked, "lay it out for us."

So, I laid the pencils out on Mr. McNeely's desk grouping them by team and showing how the price increased as the quantity of the specific team decreased. Instead of the $40 he was ready to hand me, which would have doubled my bankroll, I walked out with $125 and change and a promise to never own more than one pencil. That's real money for a fifth-grader in 1977.

I didn't admit to having a full team set back in my desk, but I never sold another pencil.

The pencil buy-out became seed money for my next venture: comic books.

Mortensen

Less than a month after but not as a result of the Sparkletts' reveal, Buchanan suddenly left. There was an ET (emergency transfer) needed in another area of the Mission, and all the dominoes eventually landed on Buchanan having to leave.

My new companion, Elder Mortensen, was assigned as an Assistant Zone Leader to me and as the District Leader over the El Monte Spanish-speaking missionaries. I cannot recall how long it took for us to figure it out, but not long after he arrived, we discovered that we really did not like each other.

Hate is too strong of a word, but we argued all the time. All. The. Time. We disagreed over what and where to eat, what work to do and where to do it, what to study, what to teach…we even almost came to blows one evening over where to park; I wanted to have room to maneuver and he wanted to practically park in their living room.

I have looked back at the photos of our time together, and he looks like a really nice guy. We are both smiling in the pics. So yes, memories fade, and usually only the good ones remain, but I cannot tell this short part of the story without acknowledging that we did not get along. Ironically, we did some baptizing, but they must have begged us to join, because I cannot imagine us being good teachers together.

My main issue was that I had really gotten on well with all my companions. Widdup could be overbearing and condescending, but he was a good missionary and I learned a lot from him. Branham and I were brothers. DeFiguerido was a good guy who tried hard…I was the jerk in that companionship, but we worked hard together. Thorderson and I probably got along too well, which may have sidetracked us from the the work occasionally. Attwooll was a big teddy bear…odd and un-hygienic, but easy to get along with. Buchanan was a hillbilly too, so we understood each other.

This was really my first time not getting along with my companion…genuinely. It bothered me. Later in life, results of leadership surveys/exercises would reveal that "relationships" are the most importance factor for me in a working environment. When the culture is toxic, I do not do well.

But when I cannot control the toxic culture, it paralyzes me. I perseverate on the discord and put all my energy into fixing it. The more I tried, the worse it got. In retrospect, I had had more success in the Mission than Mortensen, which put me in a particular mode of working. I knew that if we did A-B-and-C, on the daily, that baptisms would come.

Mortensen had struggled a little bit. As a result, he was more relaxed about the Work. I do not mean to say he was lazy, but he was not aggressive. Also, he had been out longer than I had, and for the first time, I held a senior position to a more seasoned Elder. He <u>did not</u> want to do anything my way.

Once we stopped outside of a teaching appointment, sat in the car, and argued for ten minutes about who would say the prayer before we got out of the car.

It was bad.

I distinctly remember Coach Rusty coming to the house and talking to my Dad. I had never played tackle football, but somehow Coach Rusty thought I was the next big quarterback in Alamogordo Pop Warner.

The Alamogordo Cowboys had a new signal caller.

In my first year, I scrambled left - opposite the direction of a missed hand-off to our running back - who was the eventual MVP of the league. Surprised that I was not tackled right away, the standard outcome of a "busted play," I just kept running.

Terrified, I soon became aware that I was running in the open field. All the players on the other team must have simultaneously died, because I was not fleet of foot. I was so slow that my teammates were running alongside me begging for me to let them run the ball in the rest of the way.

After I scored, I spiked the ball. As flags flew around me, I launched into an unrehearsed homage to Billy White Shoes Johnson. I was living my best life.

In those days of Pop Warner, all the Dads stood along the sideline between the goal line and the 20. As I ran past my Dad, he snatched me close to him by grabbing my face mask. Quietly but threw gritted teeth he counseled, "Don't ever do that again. Now, everyone knows you never expected to score. Always act like you have been there before and you expect to do it again."

I actually never did expect to ever score a touchdown, and I never scored another one, but the lesson stuck with me nonetheless.

Dime-Shaped Object

To make matters worse (or better, as it turned out), Mortensen had a series of health issues. The first was a gnarly in-grown toe on his big toe. We had to go to a mission doctor to get it cut and wrapped. As a result, he could not walk for a week or so.

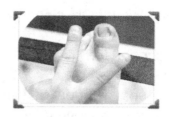

The good news: during that time, I took one or both of the English Elders with me to appointments.

Then, he needed his wisdom teeth taken out. Nowadays, all missionaries must have their wisdom teeth removed before entering the mission field. Not back then. I had had mine out while serving with Thorderson in Echo Park. Morty was laid up another week. The good news: during that time, I took one or both of the English Elders with me to appointments.

Next, he came into the living room of our pad and announced that he had a hemorrhoid. We laughed it off, but he asserted, "No, really, I have a hemorrhoid." As we laughed even harder, he said that he had tried to cut it off himself, but now it was bleeding profusely. He had a wad of toilet paper between his legs under his suit pants.

When a missionary is sick, the process is to call the Mission President's wife. Her job is to assess whatever bone-head thing you had wrong with you and get you to the nearest member of the Church who could treat you.

Mortensen grabbed the phone which had a long cord, took it into our bedroom, and he locked the door. We all immediately ran over and put our ears to the door. We had to hear how he was going to tell Sister Coleman about this.

"Hello Sister Coleman? Hi it's Elder Mortensen from Zone 7 in El Monte."

Short pause…

"Huh? What? Oh yeah, we are doing great thank you."

Longer pause…

"Well, so, um…how do I say this? Um…so, I have a…I have a…what?…no, everything is fine…but I…I have a dime-shaped object hanging out of my anus."

We did not hear what happened next because we all exploded in laughter. Mortensen violently swung open the door and ran out with the phone to his ear, "Yes, that's my comp and the English Elders." We tried to stop, but it was too much. I never dreamed that is what he would say.

Because he was bleeding, she suggested a doctor close by and ordered us to go immediately. At the doctor's office, the hemorrhoid was removed, and a large bandage was heavily taped over the hole. Mortensen was laid up on a fluid only diet for a few days. The good news: during that time, I took one or both of the English Elders with me to appointments.

On the return visit, the Doc asked me if I wanted to yank off the bandage.

Uh, heck yeah.

Hemmies

> Pecan Drive runs from Indian Wells to 25th. It was a line of demarcation between school and home. Many a day, me and the crew - Charlie, Sam, Randy and Orlando - ran as fast as we could to get across Pecan Drive before Mary could catch us. She was the school bully, and we were sure she could beat all five of us up with little effort. We once saw her beat up some kid's dad, who had the audacity to honk at her while she tried to cross the street in front of the school.

Best Decision Ever

Right after hitting the ground in El Monte, I learned that Elder Ashworth from Glendale was still in El Monte. He and his companion, Elder Collings, were assigned to the El Monte Ward along with Buchanan and me. Their apartment was on the other side of El Monte from us nearly equidistant from the Ward building.

Collings was a piece of work, and he and Ashworth clashed. It's their story to tell, but the stories are hilarious. Sadly, Collings thought I was the greatest missionary ever, and when in a room together, his eyes never left me. His head would move back and forth, up and down, but his eyes stayed on me. It was unnerving.

As soon as Ashworth arrived in El Monte, I started hearing stories: he breaks mission rules, he stays out past mission curfew (9:30pm), he has hair that is too long, he wears sunglasses (a no-no), he stays too long at members' houses, and worst of all - he flirts with every girl in the Ward. Admittedly, I did not know him well, but from my experience with him in Glendale, it all tracked.

About two months into my time in El Monte, we had a Zone

Leader council with the new Mission President, Elder Coleman, the two A.P.s, and the dozen or so Zone Leaders with their companions. After some training, we go into Zone business. The first item the A.P.s brought up were missionaries who were not doing well, and what needed to be done to help them: more training, new companions, or in a few cases - send them home. I had a keen sense that President Coleman would rubber stamp any recommendations. Eventually they got around to Ashworth, or "Ashley," as everyone called him.

The A.P.s laid out the situation including all the rumors. Apparently, he was lining up relationships with every single woman in the Ward. They went down a laundry list of things he was supposedly doing. Finally, there was a discussion of what to do, and it was suggested…more of a question really…that he be sent home.

What jumped out to me was that none of these rumors or complaints came from, or were corroborated by, any of his companions. I was thinking on this issue when President Coleman asked me, his Zone Leader, what my thoughts and feelings were on the issue with Elder Ashworth.

Without blinking, I responded that these were all just rumors, none of his companions were saying anything negative about him, and before we send him home, we should be more sure that he was really the bad boy everyone thought he was. "What do you suggest, Elder Dale?"

"Put him with me, and I'll let you know for sure," I said, looking right at President Coleman. "Done," he said looking back and smiling slightly. As I said, he really did not like me that much, so I'm sure he thought it was killing two birds.

The part I left out was that Ashworth and I were both miserable with our companions. One evening after checking on Ashworth and Collings, the former walked me to the car and begged for a transfer. I must have expressed dissatisfaction in my companionship too. "Put me with you," he said. I was shocked by that...I always assumed he thought I was a joke. I was thinking on this issue when President Coleman asked me, his Zone Leader, what my thoughts and feelings were regarding Elder Ashworth.

The interesting piece about my recommendation to President Coleman was that it "promoted" Ashworth to a leadership position. He had never trained or been a District Leader, but now he would be an Assistant Zone Leader. It should not have mattered, but back in those days, it did. Your perceived value as a missionary was based on two things: how many baptisms you had, and what leadership positions you held. For a long time, it was the ugly underbelly of mission culture. The Church has worked very hard and successfully to de-construct that culture.

Today, the message is service. If you serve, then you are enough.

The best part of the move was that it got Mortensen out of my hair. Our companionship had completely deteriorated by that point. We were barely speaking.

By the end of the Zone Leader Council with Elder Coleman, Mortensen was gone, and I drove over to pick up Ashworth with Collings' new companion in tow.

The A.P.s took Mortensen away. I'm not sure we even said goodbye.

When Ashworth got in the car, I said, "The powers that be want to send you home. You're too far outside the norm for them, and letting you go is all they can think to do." Ashworth, always ready with a retort, sat in the car very still and very quiet.

I continued, "So, I have volunteered to partner up with you, and see what you are really about."

Finally, Ashworth spoke, "So, what does that mean?"

I thought for a second, then turned to him squaring my shoulders in the seat next to him, and said, "I'll make you a deal. I won't be such a *stick up the butt* if you will do exactly what I say. Meaning, when I say it is time to leave any place, it is time to go. The only sound I want to hear is you zipping up your scriptures case."

That's it?" he said with a side-eye glance. "Yep," I quickly answered, "let's just do what we were sent here to do and forget all that other crap."

"Deal," he said in a voice I had not heard before. It did not have any mirth or sarcasm in it. He was dead serious. He continued, "You know, I have been out almost a year, and I have yet to do real missionary work…like I see other Elders doing it. I want to do that."

"Go get your stuff."

We were in business.

By the next Zone Leader Council, I walked in, sat down, and let everyone know that all the rumors were unfounded. Yeah, he was a wild man, but maybe we could all be a little bit more wild like Ashley; our lives would be way less stiff and stodgy. I testified that it was possible to have a good time living life, and still serve the Lord. We did not have to walk around like Benedictine Monks in order to be noticed by God.

Ashworth's impact on me and my life in the Mission was

Benedictine Monks

immediate. He walked in, put down his bags, and walked around as if he might buy the place. In the kitchen, he asked, "Why two fridges?" When I told him the reason, he looked at me dead pan, "You're kiddin' me." The way he said that made me feel like I was back in East Texas, not the mission field.

When I assured him that was the reason, he got on the phone and called a member in the Ward to borrow a hand-cart. In short order, we were lowering the disgusting fridge down the stairs and to the curb. That's Ashworth in a nut-shell.

Don't put up with stupid stuff...do something practical, and fix it.

The next day, Elder Ashworth and I started working hard, and he was an amazing companion. First off: he was the best teacher I had seen on my Mission. The guy really knew how to talk to people, and he had a way of resolving concerns that even made me feel better in spite of not having the same problem as the person we were teaching. It was a relief to hear his calm affect and perspective.

Secondly, everyone loved him. People in the Ward loved him. Kids loved him. Every guy wanted to be like him, and yes, the girls swooned over him. He had that confident charisma that women loved...and I did not have.

He did stuff all the time, though, that made me cringe. Like walking into a crowded room of church members before turning to me and asking loudly, "Elder, what does verga mean?" Well, *verga* is slang for penis, which he darn-well knew, but Ashworth thought it was funny to pretend that he did not know, innocently asking his senior companion in an "accidentally" loud voice. The members thought it was hilarious, and he was and is the only person I've ever known who could get away with something like that.

Every time he pulled that stunt, I just wanted to die...but again, the members LOVED him. They loved him so much that they loved me more. I had been there two months, and they liked me well enough…but being with Ashworth made me a rock star too.

After two or three times of pretending to ask for the translation or the meaning of various vulgar words and terms, I asked (forcefully) for him to cut it out. He only did it to get a reaction out of me, which he did, so he was satisfied. Our time together was the most fulfilling of my Mission, and vouching for Ashworth was the smartest decision I had made in my life up to that point.

My Mom was driving west down Indian Wells on September 30, 1978. We were listening to the radio when the news came on to report that the leaders of The Church of Jesus Christ of Latter-day Saints announced that the Priesthood would be extended and be available to all worthy males. Meaning, black males could now be Priesthood holders, and leaders, in the Church.

There is no way to describe how the earth moved that day. Even as an 11-year-old, my head snapped excitedly toward my Mom to see her big smile.

Curses Removed

Ashworth and I were comps about a month before it happened.

I was lying in bed, when I felt that buzzing sensation. It felt like low voltage electricity going through my body. It didn't hurt, but I definitely felt it. In the twilight of sleep, it was hard to wake up enough to deal with it. On some level of consciousness, I knew what was happening. I had been trained on what to do all those months ago back home in East Texas, before my Mission. I was struggling to get awake enough to stop it.

Then, bam, it was in me.

I lost control of my body, and it was as though I was standing inside my skull looking out of my eye sockets again. Instead of dealing with it right away, I lingered to experience it out of curiosity. I was different now...stronger in spirit and more confident through experience.

Big mistake.

Evil spirits take that as an additional opening or challenge; I'm not sure which. Nevertheless, after learning that bad can quickly turn to horrifying, I raised my arm to the square and said, "By the power of the Holy Melchizedek Priesthood and in the name of Jesus Christ, get thee hence." It didn't work. My curiosity in lingering cost me. I knew right away that I had messed up. I began to panic and had to talk to myself for a bit to calm down. I said a prayer to apologize for my disobedient-curiosity, then repeated the rebuke.

This time it worked.

I sat up on my bed, breathing heavily, and looked over at Ashworth, who always slept on the bare floor. Normally still, he was writhing around as though he was in pain. I jumped off my bed, ran to him, put my left hand on his shoulder, raised my right hand and pronounced the rebuke. He immediately stopped, looked at me, sat up and said, "What..was…that?"

Right there in the dark, I told him that it was the Adversary, commonly known as *Satan*, or one of his evil spirits, and that I knew what to do. With wide-eyes, he looked at me bewildered as I told him the story of what I was taught, now over a year ago, and that I was told it would happen again. I instructed him on what to do if it happened to him again.

We went out to the kitchen to get something to eat and discussed whether to tell the two English-speaking missionaries in the room next to us. We peeked in on them, and after seeing them soundly sleeping, we decided to keep it to ourselves…mostly out of a fear of sounding nutty.

We tried to go back to bed that first night, but we stayed up until dawn fighting off the evil spirits, rebuking them off ourselves and one another.

It was a long night.

The next day, we were both exhausted. We were busy, with tons of appointments, so there was no time to nap or sleep. So, normally looking forward to some much-needed shut eye, we fearfully watched the sun go down that night...both afraid to go to sleep. We sat up talking well into the night before dozing off.

I woke up first, because whatever was attacking us was walking around my bed. A strange thing we learned: if we laid on our sides or stomach, it would enter us through the base of our necks downward across our spines, but if we laid on our backs, it would just try and scare us...always successfully. Trying to scare us involved screeching and raging in front of our faces and over our heads. This time, though, I was on my side, and I could feel whatever it was walking along the side and foot of the bed...actually walking on the bed. The mattress creaked and my covers crunched with each, slow, deliberate, methodical step.

In a panic, I realized I was on my side, and as I initiated the thought to spin onto my back, it attacked and entered. This particular spirit was more powerful than the rest, so it caused me to contort a bit. I repeated the rebuke numerous times. After failing miserably, I realized that each rebuke was me dreaming about it, and I'd wake up...only to find I was still under its control, and the cycle would repeat, waking up from another dream.

I decided to try to get Ashworth's attention. I exerted everything I had into yelling, but nothing came out. I tried flailing and yelling to the point where I felt like I was out of control. I finally calmed myself, got very still, mustered everything I had, and let out one big "YAAAAWP." It caused enough of a squeaking sound that Ashworth jumped up, ran over to me, and cast it out after several attempts. We sat on the edge of my bed out of breath. I recounted to him what had happened. He laid back down on his bed, and the attacks resumed.

[176] The following night, the attacks began right away as soon as the room was dark. This particular spirit wanted to jump back and forth between us seemingly trying to wear us down…and we were being worn down. I would cast it out, and it would jump to Ashworth. Then he would cast it out causing it to jump back to me.

This was new.

The evil spirit was attacking us while we were wide awake, instead of waiting for us to be asleep on our sides or stomachs.

It was exhausting, and we were desperate.

We finally just turned on all the lights, put on some Church music and stayed awake. The fourth night, we were so exhausted that we fell asleep before sundown. I heard it coming in the middle of the night and woke up. This time, fed up, I decided to turn and confront it while it was prowling about our beds and the room. I could see it's essence or energy, but there was no form.

I yelled for it to leave us alone, then I rebuked it.

This caused the evil spirit to flee the room, as though someone opened a vapor lock, sucking it out through the doorway.

As Ashworth and I were marveling at all this, the evil spirit was in the doorway, on all fours…either crouching for the attack or trying to hide.

Ashworth saw it first.

"Dude, do you see that?"
"What…"
"I can see it right there in the doorway. Can you?"
"Oh crap, yeah. I see it too."

I remember it was very muscular…and though I could see it clearly, it was obviously not a physical personage. It did have an energy, though perceptively negative, and it was powerful.
"What do we do?," Ashworth asked.
"Cast it out again, I guess?"
"Out of what?"
"Out of here," I said in a voice that meant "C'mon, man."
"Ok, let's do it," and simultaneously, we both rebuked it.

It reacted very negatively to the rebuke, raging around the doorway, inside and out. So, we did it again with the same result.

After a few more attempts, I noticed Ashworth had become increasingly angry each time until he jumped up, ran towards it with his arm raised, and screamed the rebuke. We always uttered it confidently, but reverently. This wasn't that. Ashworth was done with this thing, and he was going to fight it, for real. At this sight, the evil spirit fled, and we sat in the room deflated with exhaustion looking at each other.

In the movies, this is the part where we both start laughing, but we didn't. This was serious, and we both knew it. We were scared. We decided to take turns sleeping.

The next day, we determined to call President Coleman. Not wanting to tell him over the phone, we simply said we needed him immediately for a code red emergency.

He came right over with no entourage…alone, which never happened.

We nervously told him the story of the past few nights. He sat solemnly still making no comment and asking no questions. When we concluded, he simply said, "We've got to get them out of here. I can feel them here, even in the middle of the day." He instructed us to take turns giving each other priesthood blessings: two of us stood and laid our hands on the head of the one seated, and one of the two standing acted as voice.

[178] Ashley first blessed me, then I blessed President Coleman. Lastly, President Coleman blessed Ashworth.

Ashworth's blessing on me and mine on President Coleman went off uneventfully, without a hitch. As President Coleman directed, we stated the authority, then pronounced a Priesthood blessing specifically stating that neither the Adversary nor those who serve him would be allowed to dwell with us in this place. Ever. They were commanded to depart immediately and permanently, never to return.

On the third rotation, President Coleman and I laid our hands on Ashworth's head, and President said, "Elder Ashworth: by the authority of the Holy Melchizedek Priesthood which we hold and in the name of Jesus Christ, we bless you to have power over the Adversary. We bless you with the confidence to feel safe in this place and the confidence to sleep through the night. We also command the Adversary and all those spirits who serve him to immediately and permanently depart."

On the word "depart," the entire apartment lifted up a foot off the ground and slammed back down. It happened fast...a quick "bam!" To say it scared the bejesus out of all three of us is an understatement.

President Coleman soldiered on with his blessing, though he removed one of his hands and placed it on top of mine to hold me there. He could sense that my fight-or-flight had kicked in. I was still in a panic but unable to pull away, so I opened my eyes and looked down through our hands and arms at Ashworth's face. His eyes were wide open, and he looked up at me like, "Dude, I'm so out of here." Sensing that we were done, President Coleman ended his blessing.

I have no idea what he said after the word "depart."

After the "amens," we all collapsed back into chairs and sat quietly for a moment. Finally, President Coleman spoke and said that he wanted to make sure that what just happened, actually just happened. He related what he observed and experienced, then he asked us if we saw and felt the same. We both nodded without comment. "Fine," he concluded, "that was strange, but I think you'll be okay now."

He asked with a smile if there was anything else we needed. For the first time in many days, we both managed a chuckle in relief. President Coleman left, and that was the end of the attacks in the El Monte apartment.

We slept so good that night.

It is not lost on me that President Coleman did not flinch to come to our aid when we needed him, in spite of the tension between us. The more we served together, the more I realized that he wanted the same things I did, and that I needed to grow up. Thankfully, he had the requisite patience to bear with me, while I muddled around and got my mind right.

Less than a year after returning home from my Mission, the attacks began again. They were not frequent, but would come and hit from time to time without warning. I have tried to connect them with significant events in my life, but to no avail. Frankly, I am now so used to it that when the darkness comes, I just ignore it. The attacks are very infrequent now…maybe less than one a year…it's hard to put a number on it, because of the way it just doesn't bother me anymore. I can't really differentiate between a nightmare and an attack at this point.

I fought them off for several years after my Mission before finally bringing it up to Ashworth one night when he and his family were visiting me and my family in Redondo Beach in the early 2000s. It's extremely personal, and I have told no one other than him, but during a particularly bad attack one night in my bed at Edwards Air Force Base in the mid 90s, I saw the face of Satan himself…an image that never goes away. I acknowledge that admitting I know what he looks like will make people uncomfortable and make me look nutty.

Ashworth listened intently to my story that night long after our Missions. Then to my astonishment, he volunteered that it was still happening to him also. It was helpful to talk it through and compare notes. There's a burden to carrying something like that...with no one to talk to about it. I mean, I could talk about it, but as the saying goes, "tell people you talk to God, and they call you *prayerful*...tell people God talks to you, and they call you *crazy*."

Over the years, I have shared bits and pieces with my wife, Michelle, but never the full story. It doesn't make sense to most people, who cast it off as some made up, crazy story.

But people who know...know.

My Mom was on the Board for the construction of the International Space Hall of Fame (ISHoF) in Alamogordo. Living there, we were in the eye of the storm of space test and travel. We spent many hours at White Sands, and I remember watching the Apollo 17 Moon Landing while we did day-care calisthenics to *Crocodile Rock* in my kindergarten class.

The downside to the ISHoF construction was it put a damper on our BMX riding in the desert.

Dogs Dogs Dogs

They may be "man's best friend," but not always for missionaries.

Ashworth and I got a call from a prominent family in the Ward. We loved them, because at least one day a week, we ate breakfast in their home…and it was always amazing: eggs, beans, rice, and great salsa.

Oh man.

On this day, they called to say their dog had died. Memory tells me it was a beagle. I cannot remember its name, but we obviously knew the dog. On the phone we could hear their half dozen kids crying in the background. They had little kids…I think all under the age of 10. The Dad asked us to come over and officiate a funeral and burial for the dog in their back yard.

Ashworth and I had no idea how or what to do, but we headed over. By the time we arrived, they had dug a hole in the backyard and had the dog, wrapped in a blanket, right there next to the hole, ready for burial. After a short conversation, we headed into the backyard.

Though the parents were natives of Latin America, their kids were not, so the family asked us to conduct the funeral and eulogy…yes, eulogy…in English. Ashworth and I locked eyes quickly and silently communicating: "What in the heck are we going to do here."

Both of us were dog lovers, but this odd scene of theatrical strangeness was confounding. Ashworth volunteered that he had prepared remarks (he hadn't), and the family sobbingly thanked him. He then offered that I had volunteered to lower the dog into its final resting place while he spoke (I hadn't).

The whole thing was a surprise to both of us.

So…I grabbed "Fido," and held him over the hole with both arms as I straddled the cut. Bent over in this position, I looked up at Ashworth as he began. He had opened his scriptures, and with a great deal of Hellenistic theatrics, looked up to Heaven, took a deep breath, paused dramatically, and closed his eyes as if to summon the gravity of the moment.

After an appropriate pause (in his mind) and in this trance-like position, he began to speak. "Fido," he said with the voice of Moses on the Mount, "you've been a good dog." On the word "dog," Ashworth very dramatically dropped his head to look at the fallen canine-warrior, his eyes filled with sorrow.

I lost it.

The craziness of this whole thing just took me over. Fortunately, none of the family saw me, as they were all head-in-hands grieving. I dropped my head too, so the laughter would look like crying. They couldn't see my face, just my shoulders shaking up and down with seeming grief.

Burying a beloved pet/member of the family is no laughing matter, but Ashworth is a nut. He's certifiable.

I lowered Fido into the hole as Ashworth completed his brief tribute to the deceased's skills: chasing balls, digging holes, eating bones, barking at the mailman, being potty trained, and the depth of his eternal loyalty. I cannot remember them all, but according to Ashworth's eulogy:

Fido had truly been a good dog.

With the hole filled back in, the Mom of the family invited us in for some scrumptious food...which is really what we were hoping the outcome of all this craziness would be. We sat and ate with a sufficient show of remorse...enjoying every bite.

On another day, we were checking on a referral somewhere on the outskirts of El Monte. When we got to the gate of the house, there was a long...very long...walkway to the front door. In my mind's eye, it seemed like a hundred yards. I'm sure it wasn't that long, but it was longer than normal. The property was unusual for southern California. It was the size of four or more normal lots. On the side of the house was an exceptionally wide concrete driveway, that I now know was likely for a large mobile home, trailer, or boat.

I was going to just walk away, but Ashworth said, "Look...the mailbox is next to the door."

Now, here's some LDS missionary tradecraft: if the mailbox is on the outside of the fence, don't go in. The mailbox there means that the mailman does not go inside the gate to deliver mail, because there is a dog; the carrier puts the mail in the box on the outside of the fence. If the mailbox is on the porch or next to the door inside the fence, you are safe to go in along with the mailman.

I hadn't noticed the mailbox like Ashley, because to me the house looked like an uninviting compound. Frankly, it looked like a gang house.

We had some experience recognizing houses that were not to be approached.

Before I could respond, Ashworth had opened the gate and was ambling up the long side walk to the door. Regaining my veteran wits, I went through the gate, closed it behind me, and left the latch up in case we needed to beat feet out of there. The delay in opening a latched gate could result in a biting or a beating.

As soon as both of us were through the gate, two pit bulls attacked the inside blinds and window in the front of the house. Yes, they were barking, but I use the word "attacking," because it looked like they were both mad at the window and the blinds. I was smiling to myself about this as Ashworth knocked on the door.

As soon as he did, both pit bulls abruptly ran away from inside the front window. Being tall I could see through the top openings of the door into the house.

Instinctively, I looked in to see if I could still see the dogs, which was dumb; I could only see across the living room to a large window on the side of the house.

Just as I was about to give up, I saw two furry blurrs...whoosh and whoosh...running outside the window down that wide concrete driveway.

The dogs were out.

I yelled, "Ashworth, dogs!" and froze. The walkway to the street was way too long. There was no chance we were going to make it. I turned to the side of the porch where the dogs would be coming. There was nowhere to go, and nothing to grab. I gripped my brick of scriptures ready to defend myself with the word of God.

Just then I saw and heard Ashworth grab the door handle, twist it and push the door open. I followed him and fell inside the house behind him.

I don't know about "normal" cultures, but in missionary culture, no one would ever dream of just going into someone's house - let alone a stranger, but that was the genius of Ashworth. I can testify after knowing him for three decades now, that he is the coolest cat under fire. He's the guy who will stand up and look for the enemy position as bullets fly around him.

Once inside, we saw something that would later be the source of a good laugh. About a half dozen young men…probably in their early 20s…all posing like we were playing red light/green light. One of them was literally making the "I'm-pretending-like-I'm-walking" pose with one arm back and one arm forward, fingers and palms extended out. My daughter, Katie, calls it the *Mannequin Challenge*.

These guys could not believe what was happening.

Ashworth was not astounded or humored. He was not happy. "YOU IDIOTS! YOU PUT YOUR DOGS ON US!! WE SHOULD KICK THE CRAP OUT OF ALL OF YOU!!!

Still, none of them moved.

Now, with the benefit of life's experiences, I'm betting these idiots thought we were the DEA.

Ashley, now measured, continued, "Someone go get those two killers and chain them up…and someone get us something to drink."

I stood just behind him offset to the right hiding my mortified astonishment, and tried to look menacing. I made an underhanded motion to one of them as if to say, "Go on, scoot along now."

What a joke. I scared no one.

But Ashworth could command a room. He was charismatic. He could charm a little kid, make the Mom swoon, and stare down a dead-beat Dad making him get all caught up on his back child support on the spot.

At Ashley's word to get the dogs and a drink, they all scrambled into action. I mean they were all moving. Ashworth went to the nearest chair and sat down. It was a cheap yellow-pleather number covered in clear plastic. Latinos put plastic over all their chairs and couches to keep them looking clean (which they do), except where there's one torn spot in the plastic. By the dark discoloration, you can ascertain how old the piece of furniture actually is…like a form of Barrio carbon-dating.

I stayed standing. This was crazy, and my adrenaline was spiking. In short order, one of them returned with two ice-cold Sangría Señorial sodas (our favorite - these guys weren't so bad). Ashworth looked at the drinks closely, and commented that they were unopened, which was good. He took his, banged it on the table next to him, and popped off the bottle cap. I couldn't get mine open, and the look he gave me was one of, "Dude, you are killing our tough-guy vibe."

He gave me his, then opened mine in like fashion.

We had barely taken a swig, when two of them came in the front door and announced the dogs had been locked inside their pen. Ashworth did not even acknowledge them. He just studied the Sangría bottle as if looking for hieroglyphic evidence. At one point, he pulled out his daily planner to see what appointments we had next.

The half dozen dudes just all sat back down and intently watched Ashworth slowly drink his soda. For a good fifteen minutes, no one spoke. I had already lost my man-card in this deal, so I stayed silently standing. If Ashley wanted to talk, we would talk; if Ashley didn't want to talk, then we wouldn't be talking.

Everyone in the room silently acknowledged that this was Elder Ashworth's meeting.

Literally, on the final swig, he very dramatically let out a carbonated-inspired belch followed by a satisfied "ahhhh." He thanked them for the soda and headed for the door. As he passed by me, he whispered through clenched teeth, "Let's go, Elder," almost singing the word *go*. I downed the last of my soda, handed it to the nearest cholo, and followed Ashley out.

We did not hesitate, speak, or look back until we were all the way to the car, which oddly was out of sight of the house.

Telling that story to the English Elders that night back at our pad was the best part of my day.

Sangría Señorial

The abdomen pains were really bad, and finally my parents grew tired of my complaining. They took me to a doctor, who discovered that my stomach was covered with ulcers. He referred my parents to a child psychologist, which was very rare in the 70s. We had to go to El Paso to see him, which was cool, because we always stopped for Arbys and Baskin-Robbins.

The kid-psych IQ tested me twice. Once because the first test came out 156, and he gave up after the second score came back 158. The term ADHD was still over a decade away, and there certainly were no medications being doled out. The doctor told my parents to back off of me; that any pressure would send me over the edge. As parents of an only child, this must have been hard for them; just to completely let me go, but they did. I had unfettered freedom. Beginning around age 10, I could come and go as I pleased, as long as I checked in.

The Hard Times

Roberto, Rosa, and Julian Vidal. Just typing their names is painful.

Ashworth and I LOVED them. This family was "golden:" the missionary term for a family eager to be baptized and join the Church.

Roberto and Rosa were fun, and Julian was the cutest kid I had ever seen. We visited them a lot, ate dinner with them, and had some wonderful spiritual experiences teaching them.

They had been to Church a number of times, and had eventually set a date to be baptized. The week of the baptism, we headed over to meet with them briefly before the A.P.s were coming to interview them.

When we arrived, Roberto opened the door and invited us inside. Julian usually greeted us excitedly, but not that day. The condo was quiet. He asked us to sit. Rosa was already on the couch looking somber.

When we sat down, Roberto said, "We have changed our minds. We do not want to be baptized. We do not want to meet with you anymore."

We asked why. He said, "We do not want to talk about it. Thank you for coming to see us, but we are done."

I know we asked why a couple of more times, but there was no discussion. Ashworth and I returned to the car and sat there stunned. It was like a family member died. I cannot adequately express the pain and sadness we felt. We were hurt with a real pain. We sat there long enough for the A.P.s to arrive, then we shared with them what had happened. If the A.P.s were irritated at driving all the way to El Monte for nothing, it did not show…probably because one of them was Branham, and I'm sure he had never seen me like that.

I was crushed.

Those are the hard times, but I learned a valuable lesson that day. On the way home, we drove in silence. Then we remembered that we had received a referral card from the mission office. This new process allowed anyone to call a 1-800 number and ask for a Book of Mormon or a visit from the missionaries. We had received our first of these new referrals, which we immediately stuffed down in the well…down inside the door frame under the door handle along with the used napkins and paper cups.

[190] We saw that the address was literally an apartment next to the El Monte Chapel on Utah Street. It was late...close to our 8:30pm curfew, but we decided to go check it out. I'm not giving a full account here. There was some conversation about, "Forget it, today is awful! Let's just go home." I can't remember who decided, but we eventually chose to go check it out.

At the address on the referral, the Contreras Family immediately invited us in. They were so glad to see us. We had a wonderful first conversation. Two weeks later, Audelino, Marta, and their son, José, got baptized.

They ended up being one of my favorite families. They came to send me off at the airport when I completed my Mission.

If you work hard, have faith, and never give up, the Lord will bless you. I have not forgotten that lesson...and I never will.

Audelino was a professional chef, and made us roasted duck for Christmas Dinner 1987.

Contact the Missionaries

"Son, Harry died," my Dad told me as I mounted my bike to head out on another unsupervised adventure with my dachshund, Wille. I simply said, "Ok" and rode away.

Heading up Westminster toward the Church, I knew I needed to cry, but no tears came. I was 8 or 9 at the time. The same thing happened when Donna died a few years later, and for that matter, when Willie died a few years after her. It bothers me.

In every crime documentary, the murderer always gets caught, because they do not show proper emotion about the death. I'm in real trouble if that ever happens to me.

It's not like I can't be emotional and cry. I can: when I drop off my kids at college or at the end of every *Rocky* movie…and all the *Creed*s. When it comes to death…nothing.

I don't know why.

J-dubs

Every champion needs a rival; ours were the Jehovah's Witnesses.

I wasn't really aware of them before serving in Arcadia, so when my trainer, Elder Widdup, started in on the "J-dubs," and how they were a pain in our butt, I had no idea who he was talking about. I never let on and just jumped on the anti-Jdub bandwagon, but it was months before I realized that J-dubs, or JWs, were Jehovah's Witnesses.

I was so curious about them that I learned as much as I could about their beliefs. It was fascinating. I won't go into it here, and you can certainly Google them on your own; suffice it to say, I had enough respect to learn more about, and understand, our door-knocking rivals.

My first area of mockery was that every J-dub door knocking team we saw had a little kid in it. We would certainly do anything we could to get in a door, but shoving forward a cute little kid in a cute little suit or dress to sugar their way inside a house seemed like cheating to me.

We also learned the rivalry was mutual. The J-dubs in the Los Angeles area had a system of making small marks on door frames (nearest the doorbell) with colored pencils to tell other J-dubs who or what to expect inside the house. At one time, I knew all the codes, but I can only remember that a small red X meant that the family inside were friendly to Mormons and searching for a religion. They were looking to poach our people. We always carried pencils in our scripture bags so we could erase the small red Xs...ok, so we erased every mark we found. I'm not ashamed of what that says about me.

Sabotaging their work was part of the fun.

One Monday morning in El Monte, there was a knock at the door. As it was our preparation, or P-day, we were in our street clothes. It was strange to get a knock at our door, but when we opened, we were greeted by a cute 6-year-old girl with two adults, who were probably her parents. She asked if we wanted to know more about Jehovah.

Sure! Come on in!

The first red flag for them was probably our furniture. Most missionary pads had one table for eating and studying and a desk in the corner by the phone. The rest of the front room was usually empty: no chairs, couches or TVs. Missionaries did not hang out in the apartment. They ate there, studied there, and slept there.

We pulled some chairs from the table, placed them in a circle, and sat down with our new friends. They got about a sentence in when I interrupted saying, "I have some questions." They sat up a little straighter. The Dad was looking around the room. A picture of Jesus was the only thing on the walls. He looked nervous.

I first asked about the 144,000, "How do you know?" They replied, "You just know, and then you declare it." So I said, "Cool, I'm one of them." They laughed nervously. I then turned to a verse in Ephesians and asked them to read it with me. In the "Green Bible," or the Bible used by J-dubs, this particular verse has been deleted. I knew it was a verse that referred to angels, a belief not held by them.

The woman volunteered to read. Looking at the page, she was somewhat bewildered that their "Bible" did not have that verse. I said, "What? It's in my Bible. Why isn't it in yours?" Now they were both nervous.

The Dad was really trying to figure out what was going on. I knew that in their Bible, on the spot of that particular verse, there was a small dash and the text was deleted. The dash was problematic: as they deleted portions of the Bible, they didn't want to throw off the other verses, so they left the numeric marking and just put a dash after the previous verse. I mean…it's John 3:16, not John 3:15, so you can't just re-number the thing.

What I really wanted to know: why did they do that? Who made those changes and by what authority did they do it? I was really asking. I wanted to know. They had no answers. All they wanted to do was sell me a *Watchtower*. Finally, the Dad said, "Are you two Mormon missionaries?"

[194] We beamed and said, "Yessir, we are missionaries from The Church of Jesus Christ of Latter-day Saints." The unison in our response was corny as all get out, but we were having a bit of fun here…it was our day off.

At our pronouncement, they scooped up that kid and sprinted out of the door. As they were descending the stairs three at a time, Ashworth shouted after them, "Would you like to know more about The Book of Mormon?"

They didn't.

 Jehovah's Witnesses

We had a swimming pool in Alamogordo. It was the source of much fun. I'm pretty sure it was the only pool on that side of town. My Dad's fishing partner, Jack Cox, had three daughters: Donna, Brenda and Shelley. They were all older and acted like they were my big sisters, which I suppose, they were . Donna drove us all around. Brenda (my cultural advisor) called me over to a record player when I was 9 and said, "You need to hear this," and dropped the needle on *Hotel California.* It changed my life. Shelley was my babysitter.

Together, we spent countless hours in the pool, riding in the back of my Dad's El Camino headed to Elephant Butte Lake, and talking to truckers on the CB radio.

Jack and my Dad were professional tournament bass fishing partners. I have many fond memories spent with the Cox family.

The Car

"Yo ho, I'm about to run out of money for my Mission."

This P-day revelation from Ashworth was completely unexpected. By this time, I knew he paid for everything himself. I guess I should have checked in more often.

"Ok, what are you going to do?"

He said, "There's a car parked in the Kroger's lot down the street from our pad that has been there for weeks. I think it's abandoned.

"Ok, what are you going to do?"

He said that when we went shopping that day, he was going to put a sign on it notifying the owner that if they did not claim the car in the next two weeks, he was going to assume ownership.

"Can you do that?"

"Of course," he assured me, "it's all how it's done." Knowing Ashworth the way I do now, I'm sure it's how Ashworth does it, but who knows what the real process might be.

Two weeks later, the car was still there. The beige 70s Impala did not look to be in that bad of shape. It was filthy inside and out, looking like someone had lived in it for a time. Ashworth's plan was to tow it to our pad, get it running, and sell it. By that time, all this seemed routine to me.

It was Ashley…making moves.

On the appointed day, we tied a rope to it. Ashworth managed to remove the ignition housing and put it in neutral. We towed it to our pad, which had a garage spot.

A brother in the Ward was a gear-head, so Ashworth borrowed some tools, and for the next several days he would wrench on that car during our hour lunch break while I tanned in a lawn chair nearby pretending not to listen to the new Bon Jovi album, *Slippery When Wet*, that blared from the open window of the sex machine's apartment below us.

Turns out, Ashworth was a total car guy…a master mechanic, in fact. The only times I can remember him mad at me was the one time I ran over his foot, and another time when I slid the keys to him across the roof of our car. Both were car involved incidents, and he had little patience for car-fools.

He got a bunch of junk parts from somewhere in town…they just appeared. I think members would bring parts and leave them in the garage. He replaced the steering column, got a set of keys made, and drove it back to the Kroger's with a *For Sale* sign on it. Within a few short days, he had sold that vehicle - with no title - for four months' worth of mission expenses.

He still had another year to go, and I have no idea how he paid for it…but he did.

Bon Jovi

Though a rocker through my teenage years, I was raised on country music. My Dad introduced me to Johnny, Buck, Merle, Waylon and Willie, and George Jones. He had a country music 8-track collection that was the envy of every beer-drinking cowboy in Southern New Mexico.

As a parent, I have passed on this tradition to my children, adding all three Hanks, Ernest Tubb, Bob Wills, Jimmie Rodgers, Dwight Yoakam, and the George of my generation.

Bad News

In those days, a missionary called home twice per year…once on Mother's Day and once on Christmas Day. The rest of the time, news came by letters. Parents, or church leaders, from back home only called the Mission President if there was a problem. My parents never called the Mission. Not once.

When bad news came, it was usually really bad. President Coleman called me one morning to say that the father of an Elder in my Zone had died suddenly…heart attack, if memory serves. President Coleman asked if I would meet him at the Elder's apartment to deliver the news.

Ashworth and I loaded up and headed over. We arrived before President Coleman and wondered what to do. Should we go inside and soften the ground somehow, or just sit and wait? It is hard to know what to do at 20-years-old. No one in my family had died yet, so I had no experience here. Three of my friends growing up had passed, and my Dad had told me. He just said it.

I had no experience here.

President Coleman pulled up with the A.P.s and Sister Coleman. Wow, this was the whole leadership team. President and Sister Coleman and I went inside, and the Elder's companion was asked to step outside. The Elder looked shocked…he knew something was obviously wrong as every leader in his chain of command was at his pad.

I wanted President Coleman to just say it…like my Dad…just tell him. What's all this compassionate chit chat. I almost blurted it out.

Finally, he got around to telling him. It was the most heartbreaking thing I had seen in my life up to that point. Sure, I had had to bury friends back home, but this was different. I was a witness to the reveal. "Son, I regret to inform you that your father has passed suddenly."

The young Elder broke down. There were questions. I sat across from him as President and Sister Coleman sat on both sides of him and literally held him up. After a time, he gathered himself, and President Coleman told him to pack a bag. He could go home for the funeral, then return. "No," said the Elder, "I'll stay. My Dad would want me to stay."

This was insanity.

In my mind I'm screaming, "Go home and bury your Pops! Comfort your Mom!" The Colemans gently supported my position on this with the Elder, but he refused. The best he could do was stay and work. It was how he could best honor his father's legacy.

Yet another example of how I didn't measure up.

In the end, it was decided that the Elder would call home and talk it over with his Mom. We sat as witnesses while the call was made. Again, my heart broke as the Elder sat and cried with his Mom over a land line. When it came to "Should I stay or should I go?" there was no question: he would stay. There was no hesitation from his Mom either. No doubt. I was floored.

With such a strong belief in life after death, the sting of this event had no effect on them. It was inspiring to me to see their faith.

At the end of my 5th grade year, Dad announced we were moving to Texas. I had no idea how it would change my life.

I went from all-world athlete in football and basketball to barely making the team and riding the bench; from competing for Harvard admission against students in sparsely-populated New Mexico to being rejected in the larger Houston area pool. From the most popular kid in Alamogordo to struggling for acceptance. Though Cleveland, Texas, is a very, very small town, it is close to Houston. The city was a whole new world for me.

The disruption shaped me…made me tougher. I harbored resentment around the move for a long time. I now see how it laid the foundation for whom I would become.

Butterfly Knife

I'm pretty sure we were tracking down a referral that day, and not tracting. My position on knocking doors had not changed, and Ashworth readily agreed. He had long since shared with me that all he had done for the first half of his Mission was knock doors. His previous companions had been a cast of characters, and the result had been a lot of wasted time. He was enjoying the way we worked: way more payoff and a lot less unnecessary grind.

We had knocked about halfway down one side of a cul-de-sac when a young "cholo" jumped out at us from the bushes. Literally. I use the slang "cholo" for this young Latino gang member, because he was in uniform - white tank top; pressed, tan Dickie's shorts that extended just below the knee; white socks that extended above his knee under the shorts; low-top, black, Chuck Taylor Converse; and blue bandanna wrapped around his head with the knot in the front.

He was holding a knife.

Ashworth, at that moment, was carrying his brick of scriptures (several books in a leather case) by the handle in his right hand draped over his shoulder. Scriptures would get heavy carrying them after a while, and it was common for missionaries to drape them over the shoulder with their elbow toward the sky. It was a common technique, but it was Ashworth's normal mode of carrying.

This time, it would provide torque.

As I started to reason with the knife-wielding cholo, Ashworth came down in one swift motion like John Henry or a John McEnroe overhead slam at the net. Ashworth's scriptures hit this early teen *pandillero*, or gangster, right on top of his head - not the crown - but where the hairline meets the forehead. The blunt-force fritzed this poor kid's hard drive, and he collapsed; not felled like a tree, but more like a folded accordion. The bottoms of his feet barely moved. He just fell straight down, dropping the knife.

Ashworth picked it up to discover it was one of those "butterfly knives" like my Uncle Paul used to carry in his back pocket while he drove around listening to Thin Lizzy and Foghat in his 1970s TransAm. To my astonishment, Ashworth picked it up and did that *whoosh whoosh whoosh* thing the cool guys could do; flipping it around; twisting his wrist; thus, closing the knife into its folded position.

I was awe-struck.

To my surprise, instead of returning it to the sleeping cholo, he slid it into the back pocket of his suit pants and stepped over the vanquished foe like Dennis Rodman over a fallen Scottie Pippin. I could see the young man was breathing and beginning to stir, but I pushed him over sideways anyways with the bottom of my foot. He looked really uncomfortable. I'm sure from a distance my act of compassion looked equally cruel, but it was not meant that way.

We took notice that the previously active cul-de-sac was now abandoned. All the skateboards, tricycles, bouncing balls, and bikes (called "bikas" or "beecees" in the Barrio) were all gone along with their benefactors. We knocked a few more doors, but to our bewilderment, no one answered.

In my adult years, I have often chastised my past self for not getting the heck out of there, but for some reason, it was all part of a day's work. I guess that's what life and work in Arcadia did to you.

When we rounded the cul-de-sac and started out, our friend was gone.

 Foghat

 Thin Lizzy

I was a good student in high school; not the best like Leanna Foote, the only other LDS kid in my high school of 700 students. I was an ok athlete; not the best at anything. I could have been better, but after leaving Alamogordo, I admittedly gave up. The coaches in Cleveland saw no future in me.

I had good friends, but it was hard to be a no-sex, no-drinking country boy who loved The Police and INXS way more than country music (at the time). Being one of two LDS kids in the school put me constantly on the defensive; Southern Baptists were not fond of us. Luckily, the dad of one of my best friends was a pastor at the First Baptist Church of Cleveland, and that probably saved me a few butt whoopings. I wanted to be a tough guy, but I wasn't.

I felt an angst to be great…and certainly more than I was.

Dummy

Exiting the shower, I was greeted with that amazing smell. Coffee cake was Ashworth's specialty. His calling card. His brand. If we had hashtags back then, his would have been #AshleyCakes.

It was October 1, 1987 at 7:42am.

No sooner had I quickly dried off and wrapped the towel around my waist, than all hell broke loose. The bathroom shook violently knocking me up against the sink then over to the opposite wall. I opened the door panicking, not knowing what in the world was happening. There was a loud banging in the living room toward the front door.

I ran that way then turned the corner to see Ashworth stirring something in a bowl like nothing was happening. It was only about a minute or two, I think, and the shaking stopped. I ran over to the big window that faced downtown L.A. and threw up the blind...I kid you not...thinking I would see a mushroom cloud.

"Get away from the window, dummy."

I went back to the kitchen as another shaking started again. I yelled, "What do I do?" Ashworth, standing there un-phased in his usual pad outfit...nothing but his dress pants...was now stirring another batch of coffee cake. He did not even look up. He just pointed toward me with the wooden spoon he was using and said, "Stand in the doorway and don't move."

So, I did...extending my arms and legs out...like a terrified Vitruvian Man, bracing myself in the doorway.

Out the window, I discovered what the banging was all about. The apartment building was banging up against the avocado tree, which was a good three feet away from the roof overhang. The apartment was swaying back and forth!

I thought for sure we were dead. When the shaking stopped, I shot out questions like an Uzi. All my inquiries could be categorized under the heading "What the?" I was truly naïve to the earthquake culture. I had never been in one. I did not know that if you were from California, shaking had no psychological impact on you at all. I did not know that because Ashworth was from San Jose, he was immune. I did not know there were earthquakes in San Jose.

Ashworth calmly educated me on all this while baking bare-chested in our kitchen. When the next shaking began, he introduced me to the term "aftershock." Like a County Coroner over yet another corpse, he offered the following analysis: "This was a big one."

[206] Later known as the Whittier Narrows Earthquake, the epicenter was less than a mile from our pad. Less than a mile! Whittier, El Monte, and Hacienda Heights sustained significant damage. After enjoying coffee cake, we drove around the Zone, checked on our missionaries, found out from Ward and Stake leaders where help was needed, and stopped to help strangers when we saw distress.

It was a DAY of days.

 1987 Whittier Narrows Earthquake

Still though, we were wild country boys. We fished, hunted, ran around in canoes, and camped.

A favorite first date was to grab a couple of shotguns, and head to the county landfill. We would slowly head toward a two-story high pile of garbage with all the truck lights off.

We quietly parked, got the girls and the shotguns out, loaded up the shells, put the girls in front of the truck, handed them the loaded guns, told them to point at the trash, and shoot anything that moved when we hit the truck lights.

It was the best. The lights revealed a trash pile covered with rats…way more than two shotguns with five shells could each handle. Girls would frantically dump rounds, then jump onto the hood while we laughed our guts out in the truck bed…safe from rodents. Good times.

Great and Spacious Building

In the Book of Mormon, the first Prophet Lehi, tells a story of a dream where he sees a Tree of Life. In this dream from 1 Nephi 8, his family has to decide whether or not to walk a narrow path supported by a railing made of iron to join him and partake of the "fruit" of happiness. Along the way, some of Lehi's family and friends are cajoled or coaxed into leaving the path to the tree by onlookers from a "great and spacious building." These evil influencers are portrayed as the worst of the worst on the earth, convincing the righteous to abandon their journey back to God.

The Great and Spacious Building is a common phrase used by members of the LDS Church. It is used to describe any situation where the world pulls us away from the Truth.

Our pad in El Monte was the closest Zone Leader apartment to LAX. Therefore, we had the mission van for picking up new missionaries, ferrying exiting missionaries, and escorting dignitaries.

Marion D. Hanks was one of the Presidents of the First Quorum of the Seventy. A General Authority. A big-wig. A muckety-muck. We got the call to go pick him up in a couple of days, and bring him and his wife to the mission home.

Being dumb but not stupid, I was immediately worried about exposing these high-level servants of the Lord to our mission's version of The Dude. Seriously, I loved the guy, but if you told me that Jeff Bridges had sought Ashworth out in preparation for the role, I would believe it out of hand.

I started quietly considering how I would get the Hanks through the one-hour trip from the airport unscathed.

What I knew for sure about Ashley is that he was dead serious behind the wheel. Driving was a science to him, and he approached the road like a surgeon wields a scalpel. He would not eat and drive. I could drive Monaco with my knees and eat an entire combo meal. He did not look around the inside of the car while it was in motion. Head and eyes straight ahead. There was no messing around when he was behind the wheel.

My solution, therefore, was obvious: Ashworth would drive.

For some reason, the van was being used on the appointed day. So, we fired up the Corolla and headed to LAX. Ashworth preferred to drive, because he hated my driving. In my own defense, I'm an excellent driver, and after knowing Ashworth for almost 40 years…he hates everyone's driving. It worked in my favor, though, in that I did not have to explain why or ask him to drive.

With the Hanks in our backseat, the drive went swimmingly until we exited the 710 at the 60. Elder Hanks wanted us to drive them through our area on the way to the mission home. It was not crazy out of the way - just a little - but we were honored. That kind of experience with a General Authority, is like driving a world-renowned celebrity.

I was completely at ease and having the time of my life.

As soon as we exited the freeway, Ashworth started jabbering like a monkey in a tree. He was tour guiding! "On the left is where we did such and such; on the right is where this other thing happened; up ahead is where so and so did this other thing…and on the left is the Great and Spacious Building." At this pronouncement he released his 10 o'clock hand from the wheel and swept it slowly, palm up, toward another faith's church building that was passing on our left.

The Luz Del Mundo Church is massive, but I never dreamed Ashworth would give it the moniker from 1 Nephi 8.

I was mortified.

Ashworth said it so nonchalantly with such magnanimous ease, like this is just another in a series of important sites to see along with where we do our laundry, and where we get good ice cream.

There was a brief moment of quiet, then bursts of laughter from the back seat. I was expecting chastisement, calls to repentance, and a speech about always respecting our religious cousins. I forgot: Ashworth was hilarious, and he could win over anyone, if he wanted.

Elder Hanks laughed so hard at the comment that he had a

coughing fit. We were all laughing now. What piece of work, my comp.

The next day at a conference of the entire Mission, Elder Hanks opened his sermon and missionary training that day with the story. He asked Ashworth to come up front to the pulpit with him while he told it. I sat in the congregation with the other 150 or so missionaries beaming with pride.

It was a validating moment that redeemed Ashworth to everyone.

Great and Spacious Building

Sure, I was more than a little girl crazy. I had an unbroken run of girlfriends starting in Kindergarten. My membership in the Church was both a blessing and a curse. On the side of blessings, Church standards kept me in line. On the side of curses, Church standards kept me in line.

I battled the urge to just say, "To heck with it," and cut loose. I don't know how I escaped my pre-Mission years with my virginity in-tact. Talk about minor miracles.

Sister Tucker, González, Badál, Calderón, and Hinojosa

The El Monte area had rock stars for members. Each of my areas had one or two strong missionary families, but El Monte/Hacienda Heights had five times that number. They were all super rock stars.

Sister Tucker had the unofficial title of "Missionary Caretaker." We were at her house all the time…eating. Her job was to give us a taste of home. She taught us how to cook great food, demanded that we clean up after ourselves, and asked about the people we were teaching.

She offered all manner of advice about teaching challenges, issues of support (or the lack thereof) from members, advice on companionship disagreements, and counsel about stuff back home. It was unsolicited advice, but we would hang on every word. We had an enduring love for her. She was our second Mom. When I left the Mission, she gifted me a study companion for the Book of Mormon signed by all the missionaries in the Zone.

Brother González was the Ward Mission Leader in the Hacienda Heights 3rd Ward (Spanish) where Ashworth and I served. He was old-school, blunt, and a man's man. He was in his 60s and had a great shock of white hair that he plastered back with Brylcreem like a Jalisco Pat Riley. His smile was toothy and wide under a thinly trimmed white mustache. He was always in a white shirt and tie.

The first time eating in his home, I got up to clear my plate after stuffing myself with Sister G's cooking, which was the best I had in the Mission…a bold statement.

Two steps to the kitchen, and he growled at me in Spanish, "What do you think you're doing?" Confused and thinking he was going to challenge me to eat more, I answered that I was taking my plate and glass to the sink in the kitchen. "That's what I have daughters for. Sit down." I squared my shoulders and said in a low, firm voice, "That's not how my Mom raised me."

He had a bunch of kids who were all looking at me like I was nuts and had a death-wish. In unison, they all turned to look toward him at the head of the table. The Patriarch stared me through to the core, then shrugged, "Gringos…" I slowly moved into the kitchen without turning my back to him and set my items in the sink. I was later told by his kids that he did not bully me like he did other missionaries, because I had stood up to him.

Brother G had been the Ward Mission Leader forever. It was who he was, and he led well. He was hands-on, personally involved with everyone we taught, and provided unprecedented support to us. We loved him. I had not been home from my Mission long when Ashworth wrote to tell me that they found him dead in his car on the side of the 405 from a heart attack.

President Badál was the Bishop of the Hacienda Heights (Spanish) 3rd Ward and the first Stake President in the area who was a native speaker from a Latin American country (Uruguay). I respected that guy so much. As the Zone Leader, I met with him often. He was the most involved Stake President I had served with. Missionary work was a passion for him. After my Mission, he was called to serve as the President of the first all-Spanish speaking Stake in the United States.

The Calderón Family was the missionary family of the Hacienda Heights 3rd Ward; they brought constant referrals to the missionaries. Much like the Gallegos Family in Echo Park (Del Rio Branch), their whole family dynamic was around missionary work. When we stopped by to eat, there was always a non-member person or family there to eat with us. After a wonderful meal, we would teach them about the Gospel. I would venture that more than half eventually joined the Church. They were the Kennedys of the Hacienda Heights Stake.

After my Mission, I attended a conference at BYU-Provo. Needing to use the restroom, I was halfway through my business when their oldest son, Jaime, pulled up to the urinal next to me.

The Calderons were everywhere.

Brother and Sister Hinojosa showed me how a loving couple operates. Brother H was the High Council Representative to the Hacienda Heights 3rd Ward. The High Council is comprised of

twelve men who support and counsel with the Stake Presidency. High Council Reps generally blend into the background of a Ward and are rarely seen at all. The Hinojosa Couple were present, constantly.

We ate in the Hinojosa home on a weekly basis. A favorite part of my week was watching the two of them stand at the sink together and do dishes while music played softly in the background. When an up-tempo *corrido* would come on, Bro H would shake his hips side to side, softly bumping into Sis H. I remember sitting there hoping that I would eventually love my wife that much, and her to me.

Their favorite thing to do was provide transportation and go on trips to the Visitor's Center at the Los Angeles Temple. It should have been no shock to me that more than 20 years after my Mission, I would bump into them at the L.A. Temple.

It was an honor to introduce my wife, Michelle, to them.

> Though I had good friends at school, my real friends were at Church. Andy Fager, Mike Tompkins, Randy and Davey Roberts, Paul Stinson, Mike Unger, Allen and Stanley Neal, Lance Hill, Joel Barber and Glen Brister were loyal and good to me. My best friend was Chad May. We ran everywhere together. His family treated me like kin.
>
> Chad and I are still best friends to this day.

Ramiro

…and María Saldaña were a lovely couple Ashworth and I taught in El Monte. Ramiro was a mechanic by trade, so he and Ashworth connected immediately. If you think listening to two people talk about car engines is fun (sarcastic tone), try listening to two people talk about cars in Spanish! Woo, good times!

The important lesson to be learned from Ramiro is how he battled his struggles/demons/vices…whatever you want to call it. He liked to drink, and he liked to smoke. Say what you will about our Church and the strict standards around drugs, alcohol, and tobacco, but we saw time and time again people who wanted Christ in their lives but could not give up things that were truly bad for them.

Addiction could be ruining someone's life who wanted to be healed, but they just couldn't shake the attraction to their substance of choice. It haunted them day and night. It was really sad.

For missionaries, there is a temptation to move on from someone who will not, or cannot, quit harmful substances. I admit to being quick to give up on someone we worked with. Not Ashworth. He showed incredible empathy for Ramiro, and he absolutely refused to give up on him. Though we never discussed it, I imagined Elder Ashworth had to battle similar struggles before coming out on his Mission.

For whatever reason, there was no way we were leaving Ramiro and María unless they kicked us out. That wasn't happening. The love we felt for them was mutual.

We ate over at their house at least once a week for months. While there, we would talk about the Book of Mormon, the Bible, and specific teachings of Jesus Christ about growth and eternal progress.

Eventually we would get around to the booze and smokes conversation. Some days, Ramiro would report things were better, but some days, he would share that he had fallen off all the wagons. Ashworth mostly handled it and did so with care and compassion. But sometimes, I would weigh in.

One night, fed up with his inability to stop smoking, I grabbed his pack of Marlboro reds from the table and commanded him (in his house) to "follow me."

I looked him dead in the eye as I shredded the cigarettes in the toilet and flushed them. I think I had seen it done in a movie. Now, as a home owner, I'd choke a missionary if they tried to clog my toilet up with cigarettes. The only lesson learned that night: I no longer weighed in on matters of addiction.

Finally, the day came for Ramiro and María to be interviewed for baptism. María had something serious in her past requiring an interview from the Stake President. I'm telling you, Ramiro and María did not make it easy to baptize them.

My lasting memory of that day happened on the way home: Ashworth got really sick. While driving along the 60, he decided to make an impression on everyone. Ashworth pulled over onto the shoulder of the freeway, opened the door, looked back and said, "Watch this." He then proceeded to projectile vomit all over the freeway. Ramiro and María watched horrified from the car behind us.

Later that evening, still sick, Ashworth decided to continue the show by puking into a large Ziplock bag so we could see the volume in real time. It was loud, violent, and visual.

The following week: Ramiro and María Saldaña were baptized. The whole experience really taught me a lesson about the worth of souls: even if they seem like a lost cause, do not give up on them if they are willing to keep working.

Just a bit of fun with some confiscated smokes we took from someone we were teaching. Ashworth-style.

> Scouting provided a sense of accomplishment. At that time, the Boys Scouts of America was the activity arm of the Church for young men. In the Cleveland Ward, there were eleven of us working toward Eagle. We wanted to get it together - at the same time.
>
> In July of 1983, only eight of us made it, and the reason was tragic.

Near Beer

One of the ways I eased up on being a stickler for the rules with Ashworth was Sunday afternoons.

He really liked to kick back after Church. If we had a baptism, then his ritual would wait; if not, when we got home from Church and meetings, he would immediately strip down to his waist, kick off his shoes and socks, and go to work.

First, he would cook a steak, sometimes with a potato, but normally just a piece of meat on a plate like Uncle Rico. Once cooked, he would take the giant piece of cooked meat into the bedroom, sit with his back against my bed, and listen to the Raiders, or 49ers, game on a transistor radio while playing solitaire.

He would eat the steak with great joy, washing it down with near beer (non-alcoholic). At first, I was mortified, but over time, I looked forward to sitting on the floor, eating steak right along with him, and listening to the game. Near beer tasted nasty to me.

I washed mine down with a Coke.

"Son, Andy and Mike are dead." My Dad had asked me to sit on the couch for the news. I had just come home from a basketball game. My mind was on getting a shower, changing into camping clothes, meeting Andy Fager, Mike Tomkins, and other scouts from the Troop on the island in the middle of Lake Livingston for a weekend camping trip. Mike and Andy had apparently gone early to set up camp. While canoeing out to the island, they were hit by a freak storm and drowned.

If any evidence is needed to show that we all handle grief differently, it happened when Andy and Mike died. My buddy, Chad, and I rolled our eyes as fellow scout, Paul Stinson, sobbed his way through the funeral. "He wasn't nearly as close to them as we were." Dumb right? Of course, that was much preferable to the grief of another fellow scout, Stanley Neal, who fatally shot himself a few weeks later.

Church News wrote a story on our Eagle pact. I think about them often.

Golden Gloves

Missionaries usually learn all manner of cultural idiosyncrasies while serving…and not just from those who speak the language. One thing I learned is that Polynesian Elders do two things well: sing and fight.

About four months into my tenure as leader of the El Monte version of Zone 7, we were assigned an Elder from Samoa. When the A.P.s called, they asked who he should be assigned to for a companion. His last two companions, they told me, had been punched in the face by this Elder for all manner of grievances, like eating the last of the chicken in the refrigerator or moving his suit coat off the bed…not his bed, but off the companion's own bed.

I had the answer: Elder Clarke-Wills. This Elder broke the stereotypes of Mormon missionaries…he was black, from England, and a Golden Gloves Champion from London (or "London propah" as he would say).

I wasn't sure how London proper differed from the London I knew, but it didn't matter.

Elder Clarke-Wills was a District Leader, so I had the joy and honor of going on "splits" with him. This involved my companion taking his companion to work in our area, while I spent the day with him in his area. It happened frequently in the Mission for the purposes of training, allowing each member of the companionship space to report things to leadership who could provide needed support, or monitoring if any rules were being consistently broken.

The A.Ps. loved the idea of putting them together, so Elder Clarke-Wills got a new companion…this huge Samoan. I intentionally did a crappy thing: I didn't tell my good friend, Elder C-W, that his new Polynesian companion liked to go hulk-mode and punch people.

About two weeks into their new companionship, we all showed up to the Stake Center for our weekly meeting with the District Leaders and their companions. Elder C-W and the big Samoan were waiting in the lobby for us. "I need to talk to you," said C-W in that wonderful accent. Before I could respond, he wheeled and headed into the nearest classroom.

We sat down, and he began to cry. Elder C-W was big too - probably 6'2" and close two 200 lbs., or "14 stones," as he would say. I put my hand on his shoulder as he shared, "This morning I poured cereal with the last of the milk when he attacked me. I thought he had already eaten, so I didn't think a thing of it. I slipped his swing, and hit him with a 1-1-2, knocking him out. I'm so very sorry, and I know this means I have to go home."

I was delighted. "No," I told him. "You do not have to go home." I then filled him in on the situation, and he bellowed, "WHAT?!?"

Uh oh.

He chased me out of the classroom and down the hall, tackled me, and roughed me up a bit…with love.

The Samoan Elder never again hit another companion.

> My parents' dynamic was interesting. I knew they loved each other, and I knew they loved me, but there was no overt evidence. They never told me they loved me, and I never saw them show affection to each other. Yet, I never doubted their love.
>
> They did, though, argue politics. Dad was very right, and Mom was very left. Dad was president of the Alamogordo Jaycees, and Mom was president of the American Business Women's Association. The only time I thought they might divorce was when Carter beat Ford in '76.
>
> We were on the way to Elephant Butte, and I thought Dad might run the truck off the road as Mom sat there celebrating to the radio broadcast election results.
>
> Their political battles formed my fair-minded approach to conflict resolution.

Super Bowl

She set the date for January 22, 1988, not us.

When we told Bishop Badál that Julio and Lupe Ballesteros wanted to be baptized on Super Bowl Sunday. He said that was fine but warned that no one would attend.

On the way home, I jokingly suggested to Ashworth that we have the baptism during halftime of the game. For a couple of stoplights, neither one of us wanted to look at the other first and admit he really wanted to do that.

In a funny moment, we both gave each other a sideways glance, then burst into laughter. This was no problem for

Ashworth, who had already planned a day involving both events.

We drove back to the Bishop Badal's house and said to him, "Why not?" He laughed and said, "Let's do it."

On Super Bowl Sunday, the whole Ward descended on the house of a prominent family in the Ward, Brother and Sister Lem. It was the largest gathering I had ever seen coming to a baptism in almost two years: two-hundred people. The Lem's had one small, black and white TV, so though The Game was on; it became a big Ward party.

I can still see Doug Williams throwing that long bomb to Ricky Sanders down the sideline.

With a halftime score of 35-10, Redskins over Broncos, we all piled into cars and drove over to the Ward-house, had a prayer, one talk, and the baptisms.

We made it back for the 2nd half kick-off, more great food, and good company.

Super Bowl XXII

> I left home the day after high school and went to Washington DC. Using contacts of my Uncle Lee Conant, I had a place to land while I looked for a job on The Hill. After some interesting tactics, I landed a job as an intern in the Congressional office of Larry Hopkins from Kentucky.
>
> It was a wonderful experience. My first time away from home and on my own. I had to make many decisions around who I would be as a person. I resisted many temptations and opportunities while I worked toward a Mission.

Music

Before Ashworth, I really did not listen to much music during the Mission. There was some classical, some Church pop music, like Lex de Azevedo, but no pop music referred to by missionaries as "Gentile music." Too funny.

When Ashworth arrived, he revealed the secret sauce: if you listen to pop music in Spanish, isn't that language training?

He had a library of Latin artists; Roberto Carlos, Ana Gabriel, José José, Luis Miguel, Los Bukis, Juan Gabriel…and ooooh…Marisela. Linda Ronstadt had a Spanish-language cassette we liked. We would even throw in some Tigres del Norte or Vincente Fernández on occasion.

It helped with the temptation.

There was an English Elder in El Monte who loved alternative, and he had started to buy records for his post-mission life: Big Head Todd and the Monsters.

Then we got a new car. A beautiful, burgundy-colored Corolla. Graebel forgot to take out the radio, like all other mission cars, when it was delivered to us. Ashworth and I rolled down the road every day and stared at that radio like meth-heads. Our method of rehab was to leave a Latin-music cassette in the player.

Late in the Mission, I got my hands on a bootleg copy of the new INXS record *Kick* that had been recently released. I was an INXS-fanatic, so for the last month or so, I quietly listened to it on my Walkman at night.

That's how I contracted the worst possible missionary ailment:

Trunky-itis.

Marisela

Mom relentlessly dragged me to Church. Seriously, I owe everything of my continued Church activity to her. Dad would sit at home and get the burgers going Immediately after church, I would rush home to eat and watch the football game with him.

My Dad always read scriptures, and he had a firm belief; however, football, Coors, and Kools were a big part of who he was.

Many a Church leader looked after me: May, Holland, Stinson, Cline, and Barber - each one a hero to me. I'm sure there were many a planning council where less than even odds were given on the chances I would go on a Mission.

For me, it was never a question. After all, as my Gram, Phyllis Rogerson, instilled in us: "We're Mormons, it's what we do."

Trunky

Lucky for me, this horrible missionary affliction did not strike until the very end. It hit hard in February 1988, especially when Rogerson showed no interest in being my companion.

Trunky is simply "ready to go home." The symptoms are easy to spot: applying for colleges, writing letters to more girls (or guys), talking about what you will be doing soon that you can't do now, and dreaming of being back in the world where TV, movies, music, and dating won't get you in trouble. I mean, they can, but you know what I'm saying.

For me, it was getting in my application to BYU. I did, and received, not only my acceptance, but the Benson Scholar designation given to the top applicants. It was a four-year, full-ride scholarship named after the Prophet at the time: Ezra Taft Benson. I was accepted as an Old Testament Studies and Near Eastern Archeology major.

It also meant letters from girls. A return missionary was a hot commodity, so when the perfumed letters from Heather Nielsen, Kim Gantt, Monica Hoffschneider, and Andrea Johnson started to arrive, I could no longer focus. My return missionary status might have even got me back into the good graces of Darcy Farr and Samantha Young. When the first letter from Kristen Simon arrived, I was done. I needed to get out of Arcadia, and fast.

I only lay out all the names to illustrate my mind-set at the time. I had been pent up from the world for two years, and it was time to let loose. Not all missionaries suffer from this malady but some do.

The difficulty in re-integrating with the world was keeping the good mission habits. After returning home, my daily scripture study for an hour lasted about a month…maybe. Then it trailed off drastically for many years. In the late 90s, I picked it up again.

Post-mission syndrome (I'm making up the term) is a phenomenon that the Church really struggled with, and still does to this day. The rate of inactivity - or even leaving the Church all together after serving a Mission is alarmingly high. There are many reasons, and I'm certainly no authority on the subject, but there is a lot of talk in this era about making sure the missionary applicant really wants to go, and is not just doing it to make their family happy.

I can identify with that a little, but I got lucky. My Mission, my companions, and my experience really converted me and solidly planted my feet in the Restored Gospel.

The hillbilly from East Texas was nearly unrecognizable, or at least I felt like I was. Even at that young and formative age, I knew I had changed. In many ways, I was just lucky to be alive, but at the very least, I was aware that I would never be the same. The new me that had emerged from the Mission was tougher, more confident, independent, accomplished, and had that way of carrying oneself that comes from doing hard things.

Baptisms in Hacienda Heights 3rd (El Monte)

Date	Name of Person	Baptized by:
21 Jun 87	Marta Estella Covarrubias	Buchanan
28 Jun 87	Sylvia Aydre Banuelos	Buchanan
16 Aug 87	Maria Maciel Andrade	Mortensen
6 Sep 87	Raquel Idalia Arana de Najarro	me
13 Sep 87	Maritza Araceli Doñan	me
27 Sep 87	Yanira Doñan	me
27 Sep 87	Carlos Doñan	Mortensen
27 Sep 87	Alex Edgardo Tobar	me
27 Sep 87	Douglas Tobar	Mortensen
27 Sep 87	Jerson Tobar	me
27 Sep 87	Diana Gabriela Henandez	Mortensen
18 Oct 87	Jose Alfonso Parada	Ashworth
8 Nov 87	Frances Escobar Garcia	Ashworth
8 Nov 87	Ana Maria Tornel	me
22 Nov 87	Ramiro Saldaña	Ashworth
22 Nov 87	Maria Perez Saldaña	Ashworth
29 Nov 87	Esperanza Ayala Garcia	Ashworth
6 Dec 87	Audelino Contreras	me
6 Dec 87	Marta Lorena Contreras	Ashworth
6 Dec 87	Jose Eric Contreras	Ashworth
10 Jan 88	Natalia Hernandez	me
24 Jan 88	Maria Constanza Gutierrez	Ashworth
31 Jan 88	Lupe Corazon Ballesteros	Ashworth
31 Jan 88	Julio Manuel Ballesteros	Ashworth
7 Feb 88	Sergio Horacio Carcamo	Ashworth
14 Feb 88	Buenaventura Gil Escalante	me
6 Mar 88	Patty Lem	me

231

Going Home

With only three weeks to go, the A.P.s called to say that Ashworth was being transferred and I was getting Elder Rogerson, who I did not know at all.

I was bummed.

I hated to see Ashley go. He was my best friend, and a heck of a missionary. He hadn't even noticed his own transition into the "perfect" missionary. There was no more messing around in him. He worked 9:30am-9:30pm, taught like no other, and conducted his District Leader responsibilities like a pro.

I was so proud of him.

Elder Rogerson was a good guy, but the mission leadership had told him that he would replace me as Zone Leader when I left, and that he needed to soak up all he could from me. He had no interest in that. He had not been out long, and was all full of piss and vinegar. Yes, it did occur to me that I was the same way when I was with Thorderson.

I wanted to call my Zone Leader mentor and apologize.

Patty Lem was a niece in the El Monte Ward's prominent family and not a member of the Church. She did everything a Church member did: attended every Sunday; participated in Young Women activities went to dances, firesides, and youth conferences...she even took the Sacrament, normally reserved for members. She had never been baptized, and it was a source of pride for her like. *You can't make me do it. A thousand Elders have tried, and failed. You're just the next in a long line of losers.*

While preparing to go home, I noticed one day that, over the course of my Mission, there had been 99 people baptized whom I had taught and prepared. I went through periods of personal eccentricity of "I don't get wet," so my companions, a friend, or family member would do the baptizing. The only way I can describe it is to compare it to Steph Curry launching a long three-point shot, then turning his back to run down the court before the ball goes through the hoop. Same thing.

Dumb? Sure, but it was my thing.

After Baptism is the Confirmation, which is an ordinance involving priesthood holders placing their hands on the top of the head of the newly baptized member, confirming them a member of The Church of Jesus Christ of Latter-day Saints, and commanding them to receive the Holy Ghost. This pronouncement is followed by a providential blessing giving counsel and direction the new member can use in their lives.

I voiced many of the confirmations.

Sitting in the foyer of the Church, about a week before going back home to East Texas, I mentioned to a group of El Monte members, including Patty Lem, that I had had 99 baptisms on my Mission.

While conversing on all the meanings of this, Patty said in a quiet, mousy voice, "I'll be number 100, Elder Dale." After a stunned look around by all of us, there was an explosive celebration.

I realize now that my Mission resulted in many baptisms. I feel very blessed, fortunate, and grateful to have had that experience. Though initially disappointed that I would not serve a foreign Mission, I would not trade my Arcadia experience for anything or any place. Some missionaries go the two years with only one or no baptisms at all. So, I feel very blessed to have had the experiences I had.

Truly.

234 We all gathered around the baptismal font the night before I left Arcadia to witness Patty Lem be my 100th.

I baptized her.

Story for Another Time

I had way too much stuff.

Two large moving boxes were mailed home, because I could only take one suitcase on the plane. Back in East Texas…Fruitvale (don't bother looking it up; you can't find it, and it doesn't want to be found)…I unpacked my boxes to stunned looks from my parents. One box full of books and one box full of clothes…anyone who knows me, especially my wife, Michelle, won't be in the least shocked by this. That brief moment of fun was followed by a struggle to reintegrate into the world.

Story for another time.

Waiting to attend BYU, I got a job with my Dad's friend installing satellite dishes. Because I was accepted as the Benson Scholar, my full ride to BYU would be spent studying for a degree majoring in Old Testament Studies and Near Eastern Archeology, but I didn't last one semester.

Story for another time.

Eventually, I joined the Army as an Interrogator speaking Spanish in a Military Intelligence outfit fighting in the Drug War.

Story for another time.

After a time in the military world, I graduated from Texas A&M University with a degree in Spanish; met Michelle, moved back to California to become a Spanish teacher, a JROTC teacher, a basketball/tennis/football coach; and a high school administrator with a doctorate in Educational Leadership.

Michelle and I would be parents and raised my daughter Bronwyn from my first marriage; a pseudo-adoptive daughter, Christina; and four kids of our own:
CJ, Katie, Jake and Joe.

All a …story for another time.

Perceptions

About 15 years after the Mission, I was living in Palmdale, California. A member of our Ward mentioned a Bishop Decker of the Spanish Ward, who used the same Chapel our Ward did. Immediately I remembered an Elder Decker who was a younger missionary in the Zone when I was a Zone Leader. I wondered if they might be related, so I sought him out.

To my surprise, it wasn't a relative, it was him! I was so excited about it that I ran up to him in the foyer of the Church, shook his hand, and greeted him like a long-lost family member. His reaction was much cooler. He shook my hand without a smile, or even a hint of being glad to see me. He was curt. After a brief, courteous exchange, he quickly walked away.

Man, that was weird.

Over the next several months, we would pass each other in the hallway at Church. I always had a big smile, and a "good-to-see-you" attitude. He would make a quick "hi" motion with no warmth and keep going.

It was really bugging me.

One night I came up to the Church to play basketball. As I headed down the hall to the gym, I saw that his Bishop's office door was open. He was in there alone, so I knocked and asked if he had a moment. With obvious reluctance, he waved me in.

I sat down across from him at his desk, and I told him that I noticed he looked less than pleased to see me recently. In fact, he looked upset at seeing me.

I asked him why.

He looked down thoughtfully for a moment, then met my eyes and said, "I wasn't that good of a missionary, and I'm embarrassed to see you, because you were my Zone Leader, and you know how bad I was."

My mouth just fell open.

After his emotional explanation, I looked at him with all the love I could muster and said with some of the same emotion, "Bishop, first off: I can't remember if you were good or not; that was a long time ago. We never served near each other, let alone together, so how would I know?!? Secondly, we were just kids, out there on our own, doing the best we knew how to do. We all had good days and bad. The bottom line is: you served. You did your duty. Be proud of that. No one knows otherwise."

He looked at me, eyes watery with emotion...and regret, which broke my heart. From then on, we greeted each other as brothers, and I enjoyed being around him.

The story of my Mission is like that: we all did the best we knew how to do. We were just kids, and a lot was asked of us. Some missionaries were great, some were somewhere less than great, but we all served.

We were there, and it was something. We became.

Epilogue

by Elder (Jim) Ashworth

Reading this book and reflecting on my personal growth over the now many years, I am feeling very grateful for the chance Heavenly Father gives us all to evolve during this life. As you've read, there were several occasions where events might have resulted in me getting sent home before my Mission was complete. Words can't express how grateful I am that I was able to stay. As they were driving me to the airport at the conclusion of my Mission, I recall President and Sister Coleman telling me how far I had come since they first came to Arcadia. Something to the effect of, *"We didn't think it was possible, and we are pleasantly surprised at your progress."*

The time I spent serving with Elder Ben Dale in El Monte was the most important time in my life. Suffice it to say, my life was not typical, as he points out, but I was truly trying to become a different person. I believed that could happen if I was assigned to work with him. I was not happy with my progress to that point and hadn't learned how to be an effective missionary at all.

During the blessing from our Mission President - the part Ben doesn't recall - is when President Coleman admonished me to leave behind the person I was before, and allow God to help me become the person I was supposed to be. That's when the whole building shook for me. It was an absolutely pivotal moment in my life. Those words would have not meant anything near as much to me if it wasn't for the day-to-day process that was already occurring with Ben's help. And I owe it all to Ben. He believed in me when very few others did, and I swear, I will never forget it.

During our time in El Monte, I came to really believe that we must have been brothers in the pre-mortal existence: that we have always been friends. He has been with me at my wedding and the baptisms of two of my three children...Colorado was a little too far for the 3rd.

All he ever has to do is call, and I'll drop what I'm doing, if he needs something.

I don't know who'll read this book, but if you do, you'll have a unique insight into the real life and times of being a missionary in those days. I hope you'll be inspired to accept yourself for who you are at this time and allow God to help you become the person you're destined to be.

If you're just getting started on the adulting road, I can promise you, the people who need you the most haven't even crossed your path yet. Give yourself some time and you'll evolve. I don't think that would have happened for me without the help of my friend, Ben Dale.

On *becoming*

Over the years, I have thought a lot about how my Mission shaped me for better or for worse. I truly believe that on balance, I landed in L.A. as a simple country boy with a desire to be something more. There was a drive and a fire in my belly to leave my mark on Arcadia. There was no part of me that just wanted to do my time…slip in and slip out. I served with a reckless passion to help people, change things I thought were ridiculous traditions, find success, and do whatever was needed to get all of it done. I wanted to leave no meat on the bone.

I'm proud of this story…warts and all.

I had the same insecurities as everyone else on the Mission… thinking I wasn't good enough, that I didn't work hard enough, or feeling I didn't have the success that I saw and envied in others. That's what motivated me to write all this craziness down, so that when you drive down the road and see two clean-cut missionaries on bikes, you will know that they are just kids…striving to help others and themselves to become something better.

How great is it that we can do that: become?!?

As with any protagonist, it's fair to ask when an actual, observable, tangible change occurred? When did I go from being a hillbilly from East Texas to a seasoned, grizzled, Hollywood messenger from God? I know not to answer a question with a question, but firstly: "Does one ever stop being a hillbilly from East Texas?"

My eyes began to become steely in North Hollywood with The Hooker and The Pimp, for sure. The new leadership responsibilities in Echo Park evolved me a little more. My experience with Ashworth overall, but especially our troubles those two weeks or so with the Adversary, had a profound effect on the tangible, observable growth. It's really hard to say.

Unequivocally, my Mission did shape me spiritually. For the record, the Army shaped me physically. I tell my kids, "My Mission made me who I am on the inside, and the Army made me who I am on the outside." Funny thing: now as an uber-adult (I just made that up), all I want to be is a simple country boy, again.

Crazy how life works.

On the term *Mormon*

For my entire life, I have been Mormon. There's been: mormon.org, the Mormon Tabernacle Choir, *We Are The Mormons* program, and many other references I could strain to recall.

Then, in the October 2018 General Conference of the Church, our prophet and president, Russell M Nelson, gave a talk that changed everything. He reminded us all of the true name of the Church, and encouraged us further to use it and stop using the term *Mormons*.

> At the beginning of his talk, he stated:
>
> "Thus, the name of the Church is not negotiable. When the Savior clearly states what the name of His Church should be and even precedes His declaration with, "Thus shall my church be called," He is serious. And if we allow nicknames to be used or adopt or even sponsor those nicknames ourselves, He is offended."

He goes on to outline the importance of referring to the Restored Church correctly, concluding:

> "My dear brothers and sisters, I promise you that if we will do our best to restore the correct name of the Lord's Church, He whose Church this is will pour down His power and blessings upon the heads of the Latter-day Saints, the likes of which we have never seen. We will have the knowledge and power of God to help us take the blessings of the restored gospel of Jesus Christ to every nation, kindred, tongue, and people and to prepare the world for the Second Coming of the Lord."

Subsequently, the Church went to great lengths to change all the embedded terminologies, from lds.org to churchofjesuschrist.org, from Mormon Tabernacle Choir to the Tabernacle Choir at Temple Square. His words are powerful and direct. This correction from a Prophet of God transformed the Church.

That said, I made a deliberate decision to use the term *Mormon* in this book. The only reason being: this work is a period piece and 35 years ago being a *Mormon Missionary* was the vernacular of the day. It has also been my identity for a long time.

"You know the principal right? The *Mormon* guy?"

I was ok with being referred to as such, and I was proud of the accurate branding. Now, after President Nelson's proclamation, and for those who have known me a long time: let me declare that I'm not a *Mormon*.

I'm a member of The Church of Jesus Christ of Latter-day Saints.

The Correct Name of the Church

My Comps

William Widdup - we are friends on social media but have never spoken beyond occasionally clicking "like."

Thomas Branham - I have tried to reach out over the years when I have had a line on where he is, but there has been no contact. I would really like to reconnect with him some day.

Denis DeFiguerido - at one point, I found him on social media, but he did not respond to my friend request.

Jim Thorderson - we are friends on social media but have never spoken beyond occasionally clicking "like." Not having a post-mission relationship with him is one of the most perplexing questions of my life.

Todd Attwooll - walking across the BYU campus about six months after my Mission I heard, "Elder!" from across the main quad. In my mind I thought, "Only Attwooll would yell out 'Elder' across a crowded quad full of return missionaries." Sure enough, it was him. We chatted for about 10-15 minutes then went to our respective classes. I never saw or heard from him again.

Chris Buchanan - I never saw or heard from him again after the Mission. We flew into and out of Arcadia on the same day, but I have had no contact with him.

Max Mortensen - the day he angrily left El Monte was the last time I saw or heard from him.

Jim Ashworth - he is my best friend in life. We talk frequently...not as much as we would like. He is a good man, a loving father and husband (to a girl he met on the Mission), and a Temple-worthy Priesthood holder. He has served in numerous teaching and leadership positions with the youth and in the young men's program since the Mission. He is still crazy, and I love him like a brother.

Elder Rogerson - although we may be closely related (my grandmother's maiden name is Rogerson), I never saw or heard from him again after leaving El Monte in May 1988.

The Presidents

President Robert C. Meier - he lived for many years in Cottonwood Heights, Utah, tending to his business and serving as an Ordinance Worker in the Jordan River Temple. He died at age 92 in 2019.

President Gary J. Coleman - not long after completing his time in Arcadia, he was called as a General Authority Seventy. While serving as a "70," he became the President of the New York Rochester Mission. He is now a General Authority-Emeritus. He called me out of the blue one day in 2013. We had a long, great conversation.

Just two old warriors sharing stories from another time.

Acknowledgements

Many people contributed to this book being possible.

The first group is everyone who ever said, "You should write a book" after any story I would tell or anything I would post or publish. The comments would especially come when I would tell a mission story. Branham, Thorderson, and Ashworth are like superheroes to my children. When Jim Ashworth and his family visit, one of my kids will invariably (and loudly) ask, "Dad, is this the guy who —." I cut them off before they can finish the question, "Yes." It didn't matter what the end of that question was. The fact is: He's always the guy who —.

Dr. Michael Matthews and Dr. Deborah Hofreiter are dear friends from my time at Mira Costa High School. I asked Mike to read the book because he knows me well, and I trusted him to tell me if the book was any good or not. He is also the most thoughtful giver of feedback. Not a member of the Church, so his questions were great.

You see, I'm trying to pull off an Aaron Sorkin threading of the needle with this book. The longtime television program, *The West Wing*, is my absolute favorite…pause while all my friends complete the eye-rolling and the "sighs…" At the time of this publication, I'm on my 57th run-through of all 156 episodes. What Mr. Sorkin did was write a show from a liberally-political viewpoint that did not offend conservatives. The administration on the show was all Democrats, but they did not always get it right. The opposition party was the Republicans, but they were not always wrong. I had Sorkin's example in mind from beginning to end; wanting to write something that hopefully expresses my faith and devotion to the Gospel of Jesus Christ but is something accessible to those who are not members of the same faith. Something they can relax, read, and hopefully appreciate; yet not feel like they are being pushed or sold something. No pressure to convert...to say it plainly. Mike was instrumental in helping me attempt to thread that needle.

Debbi was an English teacher. Also, not a member of the Church, it was fun to explain some of the stories to gauge her reaction. It helped me know what points to emphasize. She gave me great grammatical edits, while resisting the urge to pay me back for the speech I gave her after she turned in her first paper to me as one of my admin credential students at Long Beach State. I don't need to recount it here. She's laughing as she reads this.

Seth Davis was gracious enough to give the book a read, and he gave me sage advice on publishing. Both he and Mike Matthews pushed me to find what the book is really about. Is it just a collection mission stories or is there a larger meaning for people to take away as readers? With Seth's help, I was able to see that this book is about the power to become something else and how awesome is that ability.

One of my best friends and a member of the Church, Jesse Anderegg, also read through and gave immeasurable feedback and edits. Jesse's enthusiasm really propelled me. There's edgy stuff in this book, from a devout, Utah member's points of view, and Jesse said without reservation this needed to be "out there in the world." He is also a beast with grammatical edits (an engineer, who knew?) and he took a lot of his precious time to comb through the manuscript. His attention to detail made the book tighter. I cannot thank him enough.

Of course, Jim Ashworth read the book. From him I needed an endorsement on the stories as well as a sanity check. His first of many phone calls on the subject started with, "Well, first I guess I should say, 'holy crap, all that actually happened.'" Then he laughed his wonderful laugh. We've had many conversations about the book, some with his wife Judith in the background playfully throwing barbs. Jim said something at one point that really hit home, "I'm in a lot of this but I have to tell you, I knew a lot of these other stories…they were legend in the Mission after you left."

That just said to me, "You have to do this."

Lastly, I was very fortunate to give a manuscript copy of the book to President and Sister Coleman. Giving him the copy might be the most nervous I have EVER been. Firstly, because I am brutally honest about my initial feelings for him in the narrative. Secondly, because he is a General Authority. If he doesn't like it and tells me to shelve it…I'm kinda stuck. If I don't follow that counsel, it's bad…on a membership level.

Two days after handing it over to him at a mission reunion in Salt Lake, he called. "Elder, I'm half way through your book." In my mind I'm doing the math - ok: the hooker, the ranger, the dog, the other dog…he hasn't gotten to his chapters yet. All I said was, "ok…"

He then said something that lifted the weight of it all right off me, "I love it. It's real though. I'm still with you, Elder, but it's real…really…real." I was over the moon.

Two days later he called back. This time, I had just sat down to Panda Express and a Marvel movie with my youngest son, Joe. Though it interrupted our regular one on one ritual, I took the call. You don't just screen out a call from a General Authority. Also, I put him on speaker. It's not every day you get to share a call from a General Authority with your son.

President Coleman was so happy with what he had read. He gave me wonderful counsel, and made some great observations. He said nothing about his chapters.

Finally, I asked, "So President, what should I do with it?" This was the real *rubber and road* moment for me…and asking was a big risk. To be clear: I was prepared to go either way if he said so. I really was.

"Oh Elder…publish it."

Man, just thinking about it gives me chills.

He had one caveat: some of the language. "I'd change four words first, and let me tell you why if you don't mind." Um, I didn't but what else was I going to say. He continued, "I think this book should be read by every young person considering a Mission and you wouldn't want a Bishop or a parent to pull back recommending it over a few aggressive words, would you?"

Dang…I'm a big advocate for the unvarnished version but how do you argue that?

I have made those revisions, as President Coleman counseled, in the final text. I'm sure any close reader can tell where some anomalies occurred with language. In the final analysis - they are not needed to get the message of the book.

All four words are from Ashworth quotes anyway, so…

About the Author

Ben lives in Albuquerque, NM, with his wife, Michelle, and their younger sons, Jake and Joe. They have four older children: Bronwyn (California), Christina (pseudo-adoptive daughter, California), CJ (Colorado), and Katie (Colorado).

Ben has a doctorate from Long Beach State in Educational Leadership. His dissertation is entitled *Changing How We Change: A Case-study of Escondido Unified School District*. He was a public-school teacher, coach, and administrator for 26 years before retiring after serving as the Principal of Mira Costa High School for 11 years.

Ben has served in numerous callings in the Church of Jesus Christ of Latter-day Saints including Gospel Doctrine Teacher, Seminary Teacher, Counselor in a Bishopric, Young Men's President, High Priest Group Leader, Stake High Councilor and Stake Young Men's President. He currently serves as Bishop of the Haines Ward in Albuquerque.

Ben has published on numerous platforms including his podcast *Fear of Retirement* and five country-rock albums with his band, Truckstop (all on Spotify and elsewhere). He contributed the chapter on Lloyd Waller in the 2022 book The History of Mira Costa High School.

Look for his upcoming YouTube series - *The Educational Leadership Forum with Dr. Ben Dale.*

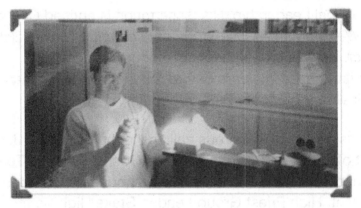

Branham "handling" a Roach Motel with a match and a can of WD-40.

©2024 Truckstop Publishing
ISBN: 979-8-9900914-2-9

Made in the USA
Monee, IL
19 October 2024